DEAR TRADERS, THERE IS MAGIC IN RSI: RSI TELLS THE SECRETS, ARE YOU LISTENING?

SUDHIR DIXIT

Made with ♥ on the Notion Press Platform
www.notionpress.com

Contents

Foreword

"Even though we do not suggest using only one indicator, if one had to, the 2-period RSI would be the indicator."

- Larry Connors, Founder, Connors Research

Acknowledgements

Nobody is an island; we all need a mastermind group to grow and hone our skillsets.

I wish to thank all the members of my Facebook groups, who are burning midnight candles to take their learning to the next level.

It is said that RSI moves precede price moves, likewise learning precedes earning in stock market.

In particular, I wish to thank The Trader's Code group, Fundotechno Investors group, Amibroker AFL Collection and Hidden Gem Hunting Group and their members & admins Abhishek Ninaniya, Dinesh Bohra & Syam Palakkal, Bidyut Biswas and Rajen Vyas. I feel privileged to be a part of these groups, as I have learnt a lot there. And the learning process continues till date.

I am thankful to Spider Software India and Investing.com for helping me prepare the charts used in the book.

And I specially extend my gratitude to Anish Thomas for providing me Andrew Cardwell's tapes on RSI. Thank you, Anish! Your help is all the more appreciated, as you helped without asking.

Who is a Trader?

For the purposes of this book, a trader is someone who wants short term high performance on the basis of technical analysis, whereas an investor is someone who invests for long term on the basis of fundamental analysis.

Most of the technical analysts are traders by default, though some analysts may be investors due to their mix of fundamental analysis and technical analysis.

Index

Introduction: Why RSI is so Magical?

1. The Hidden Challenges of RSI Trading
2. Birth and Growth of RSI
3. Real Secret of RSI is in its Calculation Method
4. The Top 10 Signals of RSI
5. Divergences: Bullish & Bearish
6. Reversals: Positive & Negative
7. Limitations of RSI
8. Which Timeframe is Best?
9. 20 Popular RSI Trading Strategies
10. Breaking the Myth: RSI Can Remain Oversold/Overbought for Several Months?
11. Additional Tips

INTRODUCTION: WHY RSI IS SO MAGICAL?

'I haven't found anything in over thirty years of work that can hold a candle to what RSI can do.' -Andrew Cardwell

All of us have some kind of natural affinity with a particular indicator, which tells us something more than it tells others. There seems to be a natural bonding and wonderful chemistry. Just like between fast friends! Different indicators would appeal to different people, so first thing we should do is to select our favourite indicator. For me, it is RSI; for you it may be MACD or CCI or Money Flow Index or WMA or any other indicator. Our task is to recognize our favourite indicator and to use it more often, as it is more likely to increase our odds of success.

Let me tell you one thing in advance; it is a coincidence that you are reading this book, because I have written it for myself! I wanted to compile and condense all the significant nuggets of information, insights, learning and experience lying here and there concerning RSI at one place… And publishing a book was just the right carrot to motivate me!

I can guarantee you that after reading this book, you will be more able to understand and appreciate the magical signals of RSI. And may be, the magic of RSI would rub on you and you will start loving it the same way that I do!

"The Relative Strength Index (RSI) is perhaps the most popular of all technical oscillators, in that it provides an easy-to interpret indication of possible market turning points and trend strength."
-Matthew Clements, editor of The Technical Analyst magazine

Let me honestly admit that before writing this book, I thought I knew a lot about RSI, but the research process for the book has humbled me. During my research I went through several books, dozens of blogs/articles and Andrew Cardwell's tapes. Then I realised that there was so much, that I didn't know! And by the same premise, there may be so much, that I still don't know. However, I have honestly tried to get as much indepth knowledge about RSI, as I could. I don't claim to know everything about RSI, but what I know is worth telling.

To me, RSI is a fascinating and dynamic indicator. Others may consider it a momentum oscillator only, which works more effectively in a range-bound market, but trust me, it can give you significant signals even in trending markets. If you don't believe me, at least believe Andrew Cardwell, who has said, **'I haven't found anything in over thirty years of work that can hold a candle to what RSI can do.'**

Most of the other indicators like moving averages are lagging indicators, as they lack predictive power.

On the other hand, RSI is a **leading indicator** which can give significant clues about future prices, if we have the ability to decode them.

I call RSI magical, because it can predict prices, because it can tell us where to get in and where to get out.

In a nutshell, these are some of the most important things RSI can tell us:

- RSI can tell us whether the price is likely to go up or down (momentum).
- RSI can warn us through divergences, when a trend is beginning to change (slowdown of momentum).
- RSI can give us trend continuation signals through positive and negative reversals (Andrew Cardwell's brainchildren).
- RSI can even help us set price objectives for negative and positive reversals (again Andrew Cardwell's discovery)
- RSI can pretty accurately tell in advance whether a breakout is going to happen in a channel or a pattern (because it is a leading indicator)
- RSI can tellus when to buy and when to sell (this was the whole purpose for which Wilder invented it)

- And if you take the trouble of using a screener on RSI signals, RSI can even give you a list of good buying options too.

Not a bad idea!

If an indicator can tell us all this, don't you think we should know more about it!

Remember, for succeeding in stock market, we need to know just three things:

1. **What to buy?**
2. **When to buy?**
3. **When to sell?**

RSI can tell us all these three things and more!

Read on for further details.

CHAPTER 1: THE HIDDEN CHALLENGES OF RSI TRADING

'The RSI indicator is a cruel mistress! She lures us in with promises of easy money and trading success, only to drain your trading account balance in a run of terrible stoploss strikes, even though the indicator said BUY! The RSI indicator is usually the go to oscillator for the novice trader when deciding to enter that first trade. There is a simple, valid reason for this: The RSI indicator is simple to read and understand.' -From Humbletraders.com article

- **Lack of RSI studies in the Indian context**
- **Lack of books on RSI**
- **Challenge of the Timeframe**
- **Challenge of the RSI period**
- **Target markets are different**
- **RSI readings differ on different softwares/websites**
- **Terminology clutter**

FOREWORD

Trading on the basis of RSI looks easy at first sight. But my goodness, it is complicated to core. The above quote sums up the situation pretty accurately.

There are certain challenges, due to which RSI may perhaps be the most complex indicator in the whole stock market universe. Most of the traders don't know about these challenges, they don't bother about them and then they wonder why RSI doesn't work for them.

This book will tell you about the hidden challenges, which are like roadblocks in serious RSI-based trading.

You see, most of us use indicators without knowing their secrets.

For example, when I started learning technical analysis, I didn't know how RSI is calculated, why it gives divergences and why it is called a leading indicator.

Most importantly, it never occurred to me that learning these things was important as such.

For me, RSI was just an indicator, like MACD or Ultimate Oscillator. So I kept on using them with the help of investopedia or other such online platforms.

Of course, back then I didn't know about positive and negative reversals. I knew so little about RSI that it could have been written on a postage stamp, yet was I humble? No way!

Perhaps you are in the same boat! You see, we find one or two tricks by reading or by chance and consider ourselves masters of RSI or any other oscillator. We don't take the trouble of digging deep in one indicator, but keep on switching indicators in search of the magical indicator.

Just remember, by digging 100 shallow holes, you can't succeed in digging a well. If you wish to dig a well, keep on digging at one place. And if you are going to dig deep in stock market, let that place be RSI. If we dig deep, perhaps we may strike gold!

I focus only on RSI and I have never switched my focus, so you can rest assured that I have dug somewhat deeper than normal (though due to my other professional preoccupations I am unable to devote much time to stock market). And another thing, I have never traded positive or negative reversals, so I don't have any practical knowledge about them. I have traded RSI divergences a lot and I can vouch for their effectiveness. Another thing, I have never shorted, so this book is written with a buyer's bias.

Now I am going to tell you the pitfalls or challenges which a RSI trader usually faces, about which he may be blissfully unaware.

Lack of RSI Studies in the Indian Context

You see, acquiring indepth knowledge about RSI or any other indicator is pretty difficult. For it we need the help of good books, lot of exclusive practice and a thorough discussion of the indicator's successes or failures in the Indian context. We trade in Indian stock market with the rules, which were written for U.S. markets.

Unfortunately, most of Indian websites and Indian books contain copy-paste material of foreign websites or books. Nobody has seriously bothered to check whether foreign RSI techniques work in the Indian context or not (you will see in the book that some of them don't work at all or at all times). We seriously lack native study material. What works in American market, may not necessarily work in Indian market.

Of course, there are several Indian blogs or trading forums or stock market facebook pages, where occasionally we find discussions about technical indicators, but unfortunately there is a lack of serious discussion about technical indicators and their mystery.

Lack of Books on RSI

Even in U.S., not many books are exclusively devoted to RSI alone. In most of the books you will find only a 10 page chapter on RSI, which will repeat more or less the same information you will find in other books.

Whatever books have been written, have their own hidden agenda behind them. They have been used to promote the author's own trading systems, indicators or investment firms. For example, Paul Dean has written some useful booklets on RSI, but they have been largely written to promote his RSI Paint Indicator.

John Hayden has written a good book on RSI, but he promotes a charting program for professional traders, with an eye to sell a particular RSI tool.

Andrew Cardwell has of course done a lot to popularise the RSI, but he had an eye on selling his audio programs; he has unpublished his book as the audio programs are more lucrative.

So you see, RSI is a neglected child of the stock market universe. And those who have adopted it, have their own axe to grind.

Challenge of the Timeframe

Any discussion on RSI can be at cross-purposes, unless you clearly spell out your timeframe. Most of the problems occur and most of the signals fail, just because we apply RSI strategy of one timeframe to another timeframe, where it is out of place. No wonder, it fails to give the indended results!

You see, what works in a daily chart may not work in a weekly chart and vice versa. Perhaps this is why we see a lot of conflicting opinions regarding RSI. Those who trade on 1 min charts are laying down rules on their blogs and daily chart investors are wondering why those rules are not succeeding.

Mind the timeframe of the chart!

Wilder invented RSI for daily chart! Andrew Cardwell preferred weekly charts! No wonder, their techniques are so diametrically different.

Always remember, the tricks of RSI which work in one timeframe may or may not work in another timeframe.

In this book, we have mainly discussed RSI in terms of daily timeframe, though at places weekly or minute charts have also been given. (We will discuss timeframes at length in a later chapter!)

Challenge of the RSI Period

To add to the confusion, RSI can be set to different periods, which may give very different results.

Wilder had set a period of 14 days for his daily chart.

But in order to get more signals, day traders tamper with this setting and use a shorter period like 9 periods or 3 periods. Long-term investors use settings for a longer period, like 21 periods or so. So neither their experiences nor their findings will be much useful for conventional investors, unless they trade by modifying the RSI periods.

Target Markets are Different

You see, there are several markets in the world. Whatever has been written for Forex Traders (like Paul Dean's books) may not be useful for a stock market trader, because movements in a Forex market are on a smaller level, so a gain or loss of 1 dollar in price is seen as heavy gain or loss. Likewise, RSI strategies of commodity traders, bond traders or like may not succeed in stock markets. When target markets are different, successful strategies are apt to be different as well. What succeeds in one market, may not necessarily succeed in another.

This book is specifically written for the Indian context. It is largely written for short-term traders (whose time-frame is less than a year), though most of the findings can be applied by day traders and long-term investors as well.

RSI Readings Differ on Different Softwares/Websites

Of course, there are several stock market blogs and facebook groups, in which traders post their findings on RSI, but I found to my dismay that these are not always reliable. The simple reason is that due to smoothening or data length mismatch, RSI readings are different on different websites or charting softwares. So when you are talking about bearish divergence on RSI, it may turn out that in reality there was no bearish divergence as such and due to the wrong RSI reading in your software, you thought there was a divergence, when there was none.

Most people love free softwares and tools. But their RSI readings do not match. This is why Chartink screeners have limited scope for RSI-specific trading strategies, as its RSI readings are found inconsistent. Of course, we can develop our own successful trading system on wrong readings through trial and error, but conventional strategies may not work there.

I would like to give an example of this:

Chartnexus reading of RSI for April 30, 2020 for Nifty (daily) is above 70, whereas in Traders Cockpit it is 59.59 in.

So if you trade on the signal of Chartnexus, you are going to trade wrong. However, if you tweak the settings and use RSI smoothed indicator, you come close.

Another example of RSI readings in 1 hour chart at close for April 30, 2020:

Chartink reading: 77.59.

Investing.com reading: 76.53.

Traders Cockpit reading: 75.51.

They are different! They do not match! Though the difference doesn't look big, but at critical junctures (like overbought/oversold levels) such difference can matter a lot.

To avoid any such confusion, for the purpose of this book, I have relied on the RSI readings of Investing.com and Spider software.

Important Tip : RSI readings are different on different softwares, so be cautious. Whenever you make a trade on the basis of RSI readings, make sure that you are trading on the correct readings as given on Investing.com.

Terminology Clutter

In the RSI world, there is so much confusion regarding price/RSI divergencedue to its so many variations, most of them quite unnecessary and repetitive. There are bullish RSI divergence, bearish RSI divergence, positive RSI divergence, negative RSI divergence, positive reversal, negative reversal, regular RSI divergence, classical RSI divergence, hidden bullish divergence, hidden bearish divergence etc. It looks like every expert comes in and give a new name to RSI patterns.

In this book we will discuss at length four price/RSI divergence patterns: bullish divergence and bearish divergence (both by Wilder), positive reversal and negative reversal (both by Cardwell). All the terms mentioned above are covered in these four RSI signals.

Hmmmmm!

Now we have got a fair idea of the challenges in RSI application and we should move on to the beginning, when this whole RSI story begins, I mean, let us know how RSI was invented and for what purpose?

CHAPTER 2: BIRTH AND GROWTH OF RSI

'RSI measures momentum – momentum is perhaps the most important factor in trading. If you understand momentum, you are 90% of the way home.' -Paul Dean

- **What is RSI?**
- **The lines and zones on RSI panel**
- **Why was RSI invented?**
- **RSI is a leading indicator**

Relative Strength Index or RSI was invented by J. Welles Wilder and he described it in his book 'New Concepts in Technical Trading Systems' in 1978.

Strangely enough, he describes RSI in only 8 pages and in the rest of the book he discusses and describes other tools and indicators at greater length.

This is interesting! Even the creator didn't fully appreciate the significance of RSI! Even Wilder didn't know that one day RSI would become one of the topmost and most popular indicators in the stock market universe. If he had known that, he would have devoted the whole book to RSI alone.

What is RSI?

Simply speaking, RSI is a momentum oscillator, measured on a scale from 0 to 100.

On this scale from 0 to 100, high and low levels are marked at 70 and 30, which respectively show overbought and oversold levels.

The default period for RSI is 14 day in a daily chart. Just check the chart given below to get an idea:

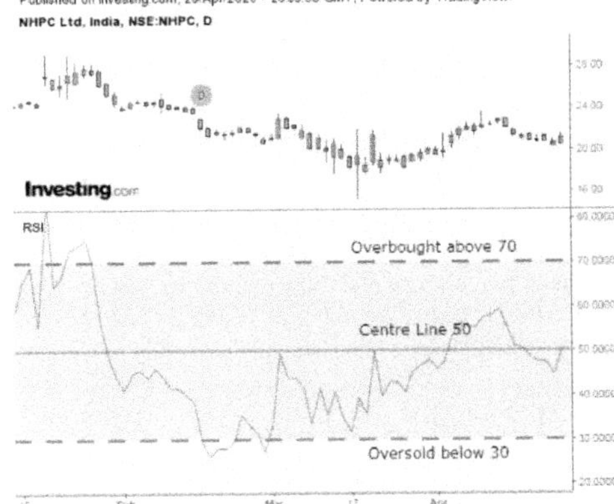

The Lines and Zones on RSI Panel

For the sake of clarity, let us analyse the above chart of NHPC. You will find price action on the top panel, while RSI is in the bottom panel.

- The shaded area from 30 to 70 shows the normal range of RSI, where it is neither overbought nor oversold.
- RSI is considered oversold below 30 and overbought above 70.
- There is a Centre Line at 50 level, which is the exact centre of RSI scale (from 0-100) as well as its normal range (from 30-70).

Now we will observe RSI movements in its panel. In this chart, RSI line crosses above 70 (overbought level). Then it slides down to 30 (oversold level) and penetrates it. Then it pushes up and touches the Centre Line, which you can see at 50 levels. And then it breaks the Centre Line.

You will need all this to remember, as it will be handy when we will discuss RSI signals, patterns and strategies.

Why Was RSI Invented?

J. Welles Wilder is an American mechanical engineer, turned technical analyst, best known for his work in technical analysis.

Wilder is the father of several technical indicators that are now considered to be core indicators in technical analysis software. These include **Average True Range** , **the Relative Strength Index (RSI), Average Directional Index** , and **the Parabolic SAR** .

Wilder was a trader and technical analyst, who used to trade stocks and commodities. He wanted to find out the right timing for his trades: when to buy and when to sell. He wanted to find an indicator, which can give sufficiently reliable buy and sell signals for a stock or commodity. And for this, he wanted to detect oversold and overbought levels of a stock.

So you see, timing of the market was the chief purpose behind Wilder's invention of RSI.

For giving more weightage to the recent price move, Wilder uses Exponential Moving Average for calculating RSI. This is why RSI is more smooth and consistent than other indicators, and tends to be less jumpy.

While using RSI, never forget that its primary function is to tell us when we should buy a stock! And when we should sell it! This is the chief purpose, for which it was invented.

And Wilder firmly believed that RSI has the predictive potential to tell in advance when a stock is getting strong or weak.

RSI Is a Leading Indicator

Wilder said about RSI, “It measure(d) the current strength and weakness of a particular market often in advance of the move."

RSI is the strength metre of a stock/index and it is considered a leading indicator.

There are two types of indicators in stock market: lagging indicators and leading indicators.

Lagging indicators follow price (like moving averages).

Leading indicators lead prices, that is, price follows them (like RSI).

In simple language, it means that price will usually follow a leading indicator like RSI, so the movements of RSI can predict what the price is planning to do.

Of course, like any other rule there are exceptions here also, but the general consensus is that price usually follows RSI.

Don't get confused by the full name of RSI (Relative Strength Index). Always remember that RSI is not an absolute strength indicator.

In fact, RSI shows the strength of a stock or index relative to the historical strength of the same stock.

It does not compare any stock's strength with the strength of the any other stock or the whole stock market. For that purpose, there is another tool called 'Relative Strength,' which compares a stock's strength to another stock or index. It is easy to get confused by the similar names, but try to remember that 'Relative Strength' compares two different stocks/indices, while 'Relative Strength Index' (RSI) compares the strengths of the same stock/index at different time periods.

Now we will move on to the real secrets of RSI.

The secret of a great dish is in the recipe, likewise, the secret of RSI is in its unique calculation method.

The calculation method is the soul of RSI, so we are going to spend some time here. We will tamper with prices to check how RSI moves and reacts the way it does.

In the next chapter, you will know why we find RSI divergences, why it is considered overbought above 70 or why it is considered oversold below 30.

So let us move on to the next chapter, which takes us to the basics: calculation method of RSI, because the real secret of RSI is in its calculation method.

CHAPTER 3: REAL SECRET OF RSI IS IN ITS CALCULATION METHOD

'The trend is your friend UNLESS it is about to end.' -Thomas DeMark

- Closing price decides RSI level
- The dilemma of the closing price
- Let's calculate RSI
- RSI has Anti-trend bias at extreme zones
- Size of gain/loss is important
- Secret of divergence is in calculation
- Technical requirements of a bullish divergence
- Technical requirements of a bearish divergence

RSI is a momentum oscillator, which measures the velocity and magnitude of directional price movements.

Momentum means the RATE of rise or fall in price.

Closing Price Decides RSI Level

RSI is calculated on the basis of closing price of a bar or candle. If it is a 1 min chart, RSI would be calculated at the end of 1 minute and if it is a 1 day chart, RSI would be calculated at the end of the market close price for that day.

On day trading platforms you can see RSI levels during live markets also, but they are only tentative and are subject to change at the end of the day. So if you are trading on the basis of daily chart, don't act on intraday levels of RSI, because RSI is always calculated on closing price of a stock or index.

It does not bother about the day highs or lows or opening (if you are interested in them, you can always look at candlestick charts). Close is the most important price; it is believed that closing price is the final verdict of traders on that day.

The Dilemma of the Closing Price

RSI is calculated on the closing price of a stock. It poses a unique problem for those traders, who trade on the basis of RSI.

Suppose such a trader gets a signal from RSI during market hours. But he can't act on it until the market closes, because only then RSI will give a valid and confirmed signal on daily chart.

Our trader is frustrated. During market hours he can see at investing.com or some other website that RSI has crossed a particular important level. But he is not sure whether RSI will sustain the movement till the market close. And if he doesn't buy today, market may gap up tomorrow at opening.

What should he do in such a case? His worry about gap up is valid; at important junctures stocks or index use the gap up method to clear a resistance or to give a message about trend shift.

In such a case, our trader should keep on watching the live RSI levels on investing.com (daily values) and he should buy the stock in the last 5 minutes to ensure that RSI level doesn't change significantly.

Don't hurry to buy on the basis of an intraday signal of RSI on daily chart, as you don't know whether RSI would be able to maintain that level till the end.

Remember, RSI only recognises Close price.

Let's Calculate RSI

RSI gives a ratio of gains and losses for a period of 14 days.

If there are more gains, RSI will be higher (with every gain, down avg comes down, though it may happen that Up Avg also comes down, if the gains for the day are below Up Average).

If there are more losses, RSI will be lower.

The amount of gains or losses is also important. For example, if a stock closes 10% higher, its RSI would increase more than that stock, which closes only 1% higher.

And one more thing, RSI is calculated exponentially, so today's gain or loss carries more weight in calculations.

If you want to understand the inside secrets of RSI, let us go and check how it is calculated (Calculation sheet is straight from the Wilder's book; I have used prices in the round figure to make it simple):

Scenario 1: RSI in Uptrend								
1	2	3	4	5	6	7	8	9
Date	Close	Up	Down	Up Avg	Down Avg	5/6'	1+(7)'	1
1	80							
2	100	20	0					
3	120	20	0					
4	140	20	0					
5	160	20	0					

6	180	20	0					
7	200	20	0					
8	220	20	0					
9	240	20	0					
10	260	20	0					
11	240	0	20					
12	260	20	0					
13	280	20	0					
14	300	20	0					
15	320	20	0	18.57143	1.428571	13	14	7
16	340	20	0	18.67347	1.326531	14.07692	15.07692	6
17	360	20	0	18.76822	1.231778	15.23669	16.23669	6
18	380	20	0	18.85621	1.143794	16.48566	17.48566	5
19	400	20	0	18.93791	1.062095	17.83071	18.83071	5
20	420	20	0	19.01377	0.986231	19.27923	20.27923	4

In Scenario 1, this stock had only one down day and all others are up days. So the trend is definitely UP.

Look at the increase in RSI levels. It is getting slower and slower, as it moves further up.

It will look like 'flattening of curve' on RSI panel.You see, on a price scale of 0-100, progress of RSI will be more sharp in its zoneless area, rather then in zones.

This flattening of curve is mostly seen in the overbought/oversold zone of RSI. In the case of an uptrend, this flattening happens because prices are increasing, but they are not increasing sharply or more than Up Average of RSI. This RSI flattening indicates that momentum is not increasing or the RATE of positive price change has decreased.

Flattening of curve doesn't mean necessarily that price will reverse immediately, but they more often mean that RSI is going to reverse; it has to because momentum is falling.

See, RATE of positive price change should be going up consistently. If it stalls, it will result in flattening of RSI curve.

In scenario you can observe that from Day 16 to Day 20, the consistent gains of Rs. 20 increased the RSI levels to 0.51, 0.48, 0.44, 0.4, 0.38 respectively. The momentum of RSI is definitely slowing down. And this is because RATE of positive price change is not increasing consistently.

Besides, RSI always slows down above 70 or below 30 for trending prices. If the price is increasing mildly, RSI may hardly move above 80. What is the reason?

The reason is that if price increases mildly, its Up Average will come down.

The higher RSI goes, the higher gains it needs to push up further. It is a momentum oscillator, so the momentum has to keep increasing to make it increase. If the momentum slows down (indicated by Up Average), RSI would also slow down.

RSI has Anti-Trend Bias at Extreme Zones

RSI typically reacts very wildly to anti-trend prices around overbought or oversold zones.

But if you are a beginner, you should know, 'What is a trend'? Trends can be broadly divided into two major types: Primary and secondary (we are not counting minor trends, which come within the secondary trend; Elliott Waves are nothing but trends within trends at regular intervals).

Primary trend is defined with the help of a trendline or a moving average. General consensus is that if the price of a stock or index is above its 200 DMA (200 Day Moving Average), the primary trend is bullish or up. If the price of a stock or index is below its 200 DMA, its primary trend is bearish or down. See the picture below:

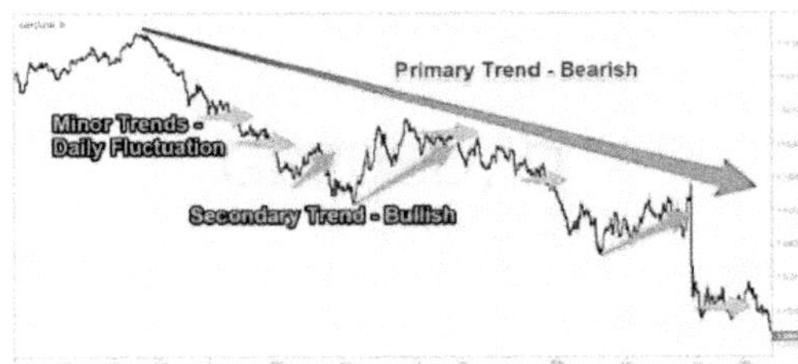

It is very important to know how RSI reacts to price changes in the direction of primary trend and how it reacts to price changes against the direction of primary trend (for the sake of simplicity, we will call it anti-trend).

To check it, now we will just do a slight change in the previous Scenario 1 and see the reaction of RSI to anti-trend price movement.

The table given is the same, which was given above. Here we have only changed the price of Day 20 and instead of a gain of Rs. 20, put a loss of Rs. 20.

Let us see what sort of reaction RSI would give in this scenario 2? Please compare the Day 20 RSI movement of scenario 2 with that of scenario 1.

					Scenario 2: Anti-trend bias		
1	2	3	4	5	6	7	8
Date	Close	Up	Down	Up Avg	Down Avg	5/6'	1+(7)'
1	80						
2	100	20	0				
3	120	20	0				
4	140	20	0				
5	160	20	0				
6	180	20	0				
7	200	20	0				
8	220	20	0				

9	240	20	0				
10	260	20	0				
11	240	0	20				
12	260	20	0				
13	280	20	0				
14	300	20	0				
15	320	20	0	18.57143	1.428571	13	14
16	340	20	0	18.67347	1.326531	14.07692	15.07692
17	360	20	0	18.76822	1.231778	15.23669	16.23669
18	380	20	0	18.85621	1.143794	16.48566	17.48566
19	400	20	0	18.93791	1.062095	17.83071	18.83071
20	380	0	20	17.5852	2.414802	7.282252	8.282252

Here price has moved against the primary trend, which is UP. Overall trend is bullish, but this day close is bearish. See for yourself, on a gain of Rs. 20, RSI barely moved on Day 19, just by 0.4 to 94.68. But on Day 20, it crashed full 7 points to 87.92, though the price difference was the same (the only difference was that it was anti-trend instead of pro-trend) .

Why so?

There is a logic behind it.

Pay attention to column 6 'Down Average,' where on Day 20, the down average became more than double and jumped to 2.41.

So whenever you look at a chart, always remember that RSI gives slow movements on trending prices and fast movements on anti-trend prices especially in overbought and oversold territories. And the reason behind it is the interplay of Up Avg and Down Avg.

If a stock is rising continuously, a small fall will move RSI disproportionately by higher points.

Likewise, if a stock is falling continuously, a small rise will move RSI disproportionately by higher points.

This is the real cause of price/RSI divergences, which we will explore later on.

Want to experiment further?

Size of Gain/Loss is Important

Now suppose, we increase the Day 20 loss from 20 to 80, what will happen in this scenario 3? We have just changed the Day 20 figures, so you can skip looking at the rest of the table.

Scenario 3: Size of gain/loss is importan								
1	2	3	4	5	6	7	8	9
Date	Close	Up	Down	Up Avg	Down Avg	5/6'	1+(7)'	1
1	80							
2	100	20	0					
3	120	20	0					
4	140	20	0					
5	160	20	0					
6	180	20	0					
7	200	20	0					
8	220	20	0					
9	240	20	0					
10	260	20	0					
11	240	0	20					
12	260	20	0					
13	280	20	0					
14	300	20	0					
15	320	20	0	18.57143	1.428571	13	14	7
16	340	20	0	18.67347	1.326531	14.07692	15.07692	6
17	360	20	0	18.76822	1.231778	15.23669	16.23669	6
18	380	20	0	18.85621	1.143794	16.48566	17.48566	5
19	400	20	0	18.93791	1.062095	17.83071	18.83071	5

20	320	0	80	17.5852	6.700516	2.624454	3.624454	2

See the jump in down average (it jumps whooping six times) and corresponding big change in RSI levels. RSI falls no less than 22 points; can you believe it? It happened because anti-trend momentum became stronger sharply. And RSI is a momentum oscillator.

So remember, the quantum or the size of fall is important. And it is also important whether the price is moving in the direction of the trend or against it.

And don't forget to check Day 15 and Day 20 figures. Price on both these days is the same, i.e. 320, but see the difference in RSI levels!

Interesting Fact

Can a stock touch 100 level of RSI? Yes, if it is continuously on upper circuit since its listing, as its Down Average would be 0. For example, Ruchi Soya has RSI levels of 100 since February 2020, because after its relisting there is not a single Down Day here, so Down Avg is 0.

The price of Ruchi Soya was around 35 in February 2020, but due to continuous upper circuits, it zoomed to 480 levels as on May 6, 2020 and the upper circuit button is still on.

Secret of Divergence is in Calculation

Unless you happen to have the tastes of Warren Buffett or Charlie Munger, spreadsheets may seem boring to you, so excuse me but I would like to show just one more spreadsheet, which will show you how a divergence happens between RSI and price.

In simple language, divergence means that price and RSI are going in opposite directions; either price is going up and RSI is declining (around overbought levels) or price is going down and RSI is increasing (around oversold levels).

In technical terms, there are more requirements (For less confusion, I am giving a bullish trend scenario; you can apply it to bearish trend scenario).

Technical Requirements of a Bullish Divergence

1. Price makes a new recent high P1 (not all time high, but the top peak on the recent chart). RSI also makes a new high R1.
2. Price gives at least one or more than one red candle in the opposite direction P2 (that means bearish candle in a bullish trend).
3. Price makes another new high P3, above its recent high.
4. RSI fails to reach or cross the level of its previous high R1.

This is RSI Bullish Divergence in a nutshell.

Technical Requirements of a Bearish Divergence

1. Price makes a new recent low P1 (not all time low, but the lowest valley on the recent chart). RSI also makes a new low R1.
2. Price gives at least one or more than one green candle in the opposite direction P2 (that means bullish candle in a bearish trend).
3. Price makes another new low P3, below its recent low.
4. RSI fails to reach or cross the level of its previous low R1.

Now look for yourself, how a price/RSI divergence takes place in the spreadsheet.

Scenario 4: Why Price/RSI Divergence happens?							
1	2	3	4	5	6	7	8
Date	Close	Up	Down	Up Avg	Down Avg	5/6'	1+(7)'
1	80						
2	100	20	0				
3	120	20	0				
4	140	20	0				

5	160	20	0				
6	180	20	0				
7	200	20	0				
8	220	20	0				
9	240	20	0				
10	260	20	0				
11	240	0	20				
12	260	20	0				
13	280	20	0				
14	300	20	0				
15	320	20	0	18.57143	1.428571	13	14
16	340	20	0	18.67347	1.326531	14.07692	15.07692
17	320	0	20	17.33965	2.66035	6.517808	7.517808
18	350	30	0	18.24396	2.470325	7.385248	8.385248
19	320	0	30	16.94082	4.43673	3.818312	4.818312
20	360	40	0	18.58791	4.119821	4.511824	5.511824

In the above spreadsheet 'Scenario 4', you can see at a glance that the stock is in a clear uptrend and price is rising most of the days. No wonder, its RSI is above 90 on 15th day.

On Day 16, the stock gains Rs. 20 and makes a new high of 340. Check the RSI level (93.36), as it would be useful when we discuss RSI divergence. As the stock is in an uptrend, there is not much impact on the Up Average, so RSI gives only a modest increase of 0.51.

On Day 17, the price declines by Rs. 20 (the same price difference as on Day 16), but as this movement is against the prevailing trend, so it makes a significant impact on the Down Average, that's why RSI declines by full 7 points. Look at Column 6 'Down Average.' On Day 16, it was merely 1.32, but doubled on Day 17. No wonder, RSI gave such a drastic reaction!

On Day 18, price increases by Rs. 30 and the stock makes a new high of 350. Check RSI levels (88.07); it is less than Day 16 RSI level. The price has made a new high, but RSI didn't make a new high and gave a lesser reading. This is Divergence No. 1. By the way, price/RSI divergences occur due to disproportionate anti-trend reactions of RSI.

On Day 19, price declines by Rs. 30 and look! Column 6 'Down Average' increases substantially and hence RSI gives a sharp reaction by declining a whooping 9 points.

On Day 20, the price increases by 40 and stock makes a new high of 360. However check RSI levels here in the last column (it is 81.85). Here stock has made a new high, but RSI didn't make a new high, so here we have Divergence no. 2.

As they say, a picture is more than a thousand words, so I am here giving two charts related to Scenario 4: RSI Divergence. They will tell you the whole story at a single glance.

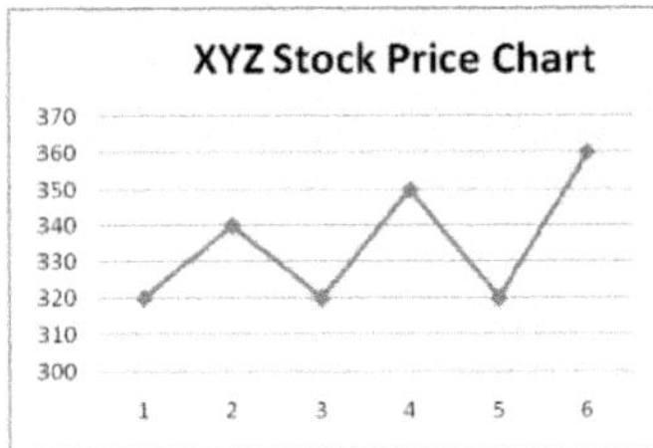

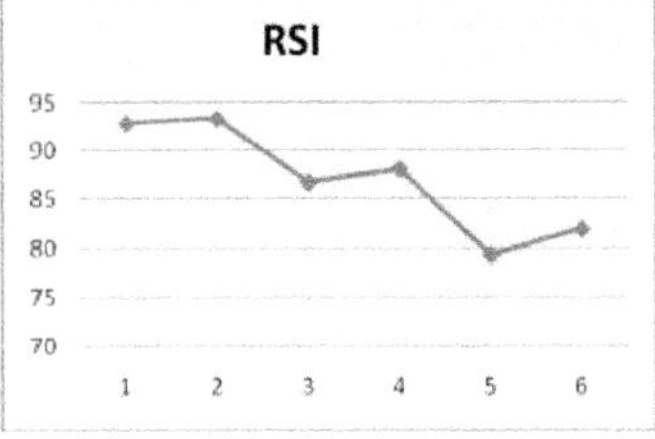

Now check the three new highs in the table below to understand the concept of divergence more clearly (and remember that a bearish candle exists between these new highs according to technical requirements).

RSI Bullish Divergence	20-40 levels

Important Tip:

If you want to compare the movements of price and RSI more accurately, don't look at the candlestick chart, but at the LINE chart of the stock.

In a line chart, it would be easier to compare the slopes and angles of both the lines.

When you will compare one line (price) with another line (RSI), it would be like comparing oranges to oranges.

When you compare candlesticks with RSI line, it is like comparing cucumber with oranges.

Note : Candlesticks have their own significance, but for the purpose of RSI comparison, it is somewhat better to check line charts also.

Like this:

If you observe the price line and RSI line in the above chart, you will notice at a glance that there is bullish divergence at bottom. RSI has peaked before price and given a signal of trend change.

After understanding the typical RSI calculation methodology, which clarifies the divergence signal, let us move on to the next chapter, where we will briefly discuss other significant signals given by RSI.

CHAPTER 4: THE TOP 10 SIGNALS OF RSI

"Whether you are a seasoned trader, or a brand new trader, learning the key concepts of the RSI, Relative Strength Index, is perhaps the most important thing you can do to advance your trading career." -Paul Dean

1. **Tops and Bottoms**
2. **Failure Swings**
3. **Support and Resistance**
4. **Centreline Crossover**
5. **Range Shift (Trend change signal)**
6. **Channels & Trendlines**
7. **Chart patterns like Triangles, Head & Shoulders, Iinverted H&S etc.**
8. **9 day RSI Average Crossover**
9. **Divergences: Bullish and Bearish**
10. **Reversals: Positive and Negative**

In this chapter, we will discuss the signals of RSI, which can be used for trading purposes:

1. **Tops and Bottoms**
2. **Failure Swings**
3. **Support and Resistance**
4. **Centreline Crossover**
5. **Range Shift (Trend change signal)**
6. **Channels & Trendlines**
7. **Chart patterns like Triangles, Head & Shoulders, Iinverted H&S etc.**
8. **9 day RSI Average Crossover**
9. **Divergences: Bullish and Bearish**
10. **Reversals: Positive and Negative**

Let us now briefly discuss them with the help of charts.

1. Tops and Bottoms (top at 70 and bottom at 30)

According to Wilder, tops and bottoms are indicated when the RSI goes above 70 or below 30. It is called Vanilla trading strategy, which has been discussed in Chapter 9 .

According to Wilder, 'The Index will usually top out or bottom out before the actual market top or bottom, giving an indication that a reversal or at least a significant reaction is imminent.'

RSI gives an indication of overbought and oversold conditions, so the simplest thing in the world would be to buy a stock, when its RSI reverses from 30 levels and sell it when its RSI reverses from 70 levels. Simple as clockwork!

Yet it is not that simple. RSI doesn't dutifully travel straight to the opposite line, but at times it reverses in between to touch the same line again.

As you can see in the chart given below, price is in the downtrend. Pay attention to RSI in the bottom panel. It regularly shuttles from oversold zone (30) to overbought zone (70), though at times it reverses its course in between. Here, the dotted line on the top of RSI panel indicates 70 level and dotted line on the bottom of the panel indicates 30 level.

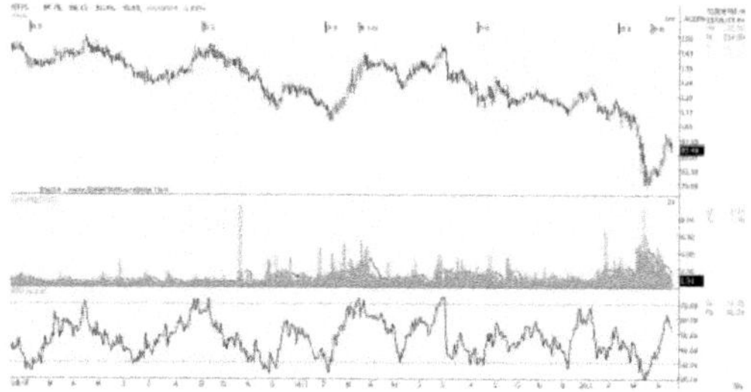

2. Failure Swings

When RSI does not exceed its previous high at overbought or oversold levels, it is called a failure swing. Here RSI makes a slanted M (overbought level) or slanted W (oversold level) like pattern. In technical terms it makes a sort of double top or double bottom.

Failure Swing is very similar to divergence.

Wilder has pointed out that whenever the RSI gives a failure swing at the top and falls down below its preceding valley, the stock can be sold or rather short-sold.

Likewise, whenever the RSI gives a failure swing at the bottom and rises above its preceding peak, the stock can be bought.

Wilder has laid down rules about trading failure swings in his book, as can be seen in the picture given below.

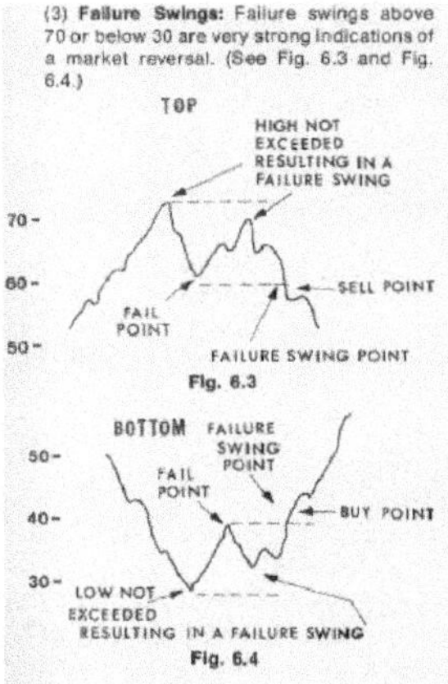

(3) **Failure Swings:** Failure swings above 70 or below 30 are very strong indications of a market reversal. (See Fig. 6.3 and Fig. 6.4.)

Fig. 6.3

Fig. 6.4

Failure swing signal is confirmed, when RSI drops below the valley in M-formation or it rises above its preceding peak in W-formation.

Failure swing is considered more significant, when it takes place within the oversold or overbought zones.

Note: However, common sense tells us that failure swings often happen outside oversold/overbought zones. Usually the first peak/valley is inside the oversold/overbought zone and the second peak or valley is made outside the zone. (As I have already told, this is similar to divergence and the failure swing is the way to trade a RSI divergence. (There have been several experts including Cardwell and Hayden and several others, who claim that RSI divergences can't be traded. They failed to see that divergences can be traded and failure swing is the way to trade them.)

Failure swings are rather a part of divergence and Wilder is using failure swing to confirm the divergence. Divergences can fail, if the RSI retreats from the zone, but turns back soon to enter the zone and exceed the previous high/low. Wilder is in fact saying that if failure swing is confirmed in the above manner, the risk of RSI's turning back is less and it should be expected to touch its opposite zone.

As John Hayden points out, 'A failure swing occurs when there is either a bearish or bullish divergence… The failure swing is believed to "confirm" that a market reversal is valid.'

3. Support and Resistance

Support and Resistance areas often show up on RSI before they appear on price panel. By drawing trendlines and channels on RSI line, we can recognise support and resistance areas on price chart.

- For drawing a resistance trendline, draw a line connecting recent highs of RSI.
- For drawing a support trendline, draw a line connecting recent lows of RSI.

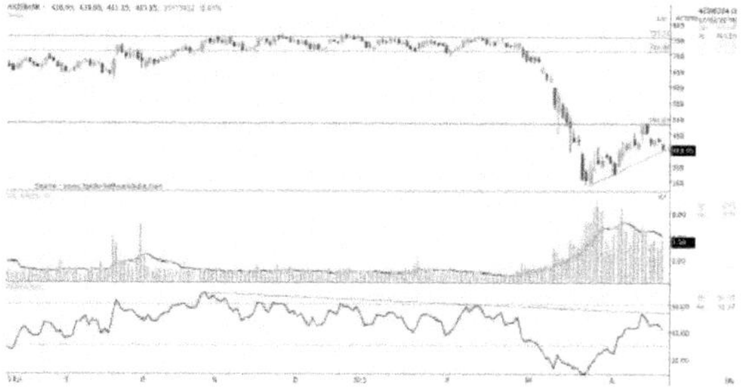

In the above chart, RSI resistance line has clearly marked the level, where price would stop increasing and reverse.
Note: It is very strange that an indicator's trendline can plot support and resistance areas. You see, most of the traders don't draw trendlines on RSI panel. Besides, trendlines are highly subjective and not at all objective like horizontal price levels. So it is quite amazing, why and how a support or resistance line on RSI can predict the future price movements of a stock. Quite incredible!

4. Centreline Crossover

If RSI line crosses the centreline from below to the upside, it means that the average gains are exceeding the average losses now. It signals a bullish momentum shift and this is why it is considered to be a good buy signal.

On the other hand, if RSI line crosses the centreline from above to the downside, it means that the average losses are exceeding the average gains. It signals a bearish momentum shift and this is why it is considered to be a good sell signal.

RSI line of 50 is considered to be a support and resistance in itself.

When RSI rallies above 50, it is considered a bullish confirmation; when it falls below 50, it is seen as a bearish confirmation.

50 is considered to be the middle territory of RSI, as it falls in the exact middle of 0-100 and 30-70 range. However, in the case of Cardwell's range shifts 50 level ceases to be the exact middle, as you will see in the next point.

In bull market, the centreline (50) provides multiple low-risk buying opportunities as the RSI spends most of the time between 50-70 range.

In bear market, the centreline (50) provides multiple shorting opportunities as RSI spend most of the time between 50-30 range.

5. Range Shift (Trend change signal)

Wilder's normal range for RSI was 30-70; when RSI was below 30, it was considered oversold; when RSI was above 70, it was considered overbought.

However, Andrew Cardwell modified the original theory by proclaiming that this 30-70 range is not universal.

Cardwell noticed that in uptrends RSI usually maintains levels of 40-80, while in downtrends it maintains levels of 20-60. Cardwell observed that when securities change from uptrend to downtrend and vice versa, the RSI will undergo a "range shift."

- Normal Range: 30-70

- Bull Range: 40-80
- Bear Range: 20-60

This idea is psychologically tenable.

Range shift takes place due to fear and greed.

In bull market, when a stock corrects, the left-out investors turn greedy and rush in early to buy the stock and move it up, so RSI doesn't fall to its normal range of 30.

And in a bull market, when a stock reaches the overbought levels of 70, nobody is in a hurry to book profits, as the stock is rising every day. When there is no serious selling, RSI goes on to touch 80 levels, as its Up average is going consistently up and Down average is going consistently down (remember our calculation sheets).

As Andrew Cardwell puts it, 'So the RSI to me is an ideal indicator because it's incorporating not only price and momentum but it can also be used as a sentiment tool to see when most people are bullish, they get excited, it's going to go through the 70 level. When it corrects, it's not going to correct all the way down to 30. It will come near 40 and those who missed the train first out of the station are more apt to jump on it because by then you've established enough of a trend.'

In the bear market, people are more afraid to buy, so they don't purchase the stock at 30 levels; there is no hurry, as the stock is falling every day. You see, here Down Average is increasing every day and Up average is going down, so RSI goes below 30 easily.

In a bear market, when RSI rises and reaches near 60 level, traders are overcome with fear that its price may fall any time, so they want to book profits in a hurry, otherwise they will miss the boat.

As Constance Brown puts it, 'The general rule to follow for a bear market is that RSI will oscillate within a range of 20 to 30 at the low end of the scale up to an upper resistance zone of 55 to 65. This is true regardless of market or time horizon.'

As I have said, theoretically the concept of range shift is all right.

However, range shift doesn't work much in Indian market, at least in the daily charts of Nifty or its 50 companies. We observe that in almost all of the daily charts, RSI regularly touches 30 in bull markets too. And it does not touch 80 so often in daily chart.

May be, Cardwell or Constance Brown were talking about another timeframe (weekly or monthly charts instead of daily charts), or may be, they were talking about another market (forex or commodity instead of stocks).

Remember, monthly charts are slow. In April 2020, Nifty monthly RSI was 31.92 (after the 30% quick crash) and it was the lowest reading after 1996. Even during 2008 bear market, the lowest reading of Nifty monthly RSI was 35.47, so this range shift of Cardwell doesn't apply there too.

Cardwell's research might have shown range shift working in certain markets, but it seems that Indian stock market still follows Wilder and his 30-70 rule in daily timeframe.

Cardwell's concept of range shift may be true of lesser time frames or minute charts (I myself have done a trade once on this basis in 1 min chart).

In the daily charts of Nifty stocks, the evidence of range shift was lacking; they kept on shuttling between 70 and 30 almost regularly, whether they were in uptrend or downtrend.

Perhaps the logic behind the range shift is that a stock turns bearish due to bearish divergence of RSI, which should necessarily take place below the previous top and therefore 60 is the ideal place for RSI to turn back.

Important Finding: In my research on daily charts of Nifty stocks, I observed that during downtrends, stocks dip deeper below 30 and during uptrends stocks tend to cross far above 70. It is not necessary to touch 20 or 80 levels, but they tend to go deeper than usual in the overbought/oversold zones.

If a stock is in downtrend, it is obviously weak. Reason is that there is more selling going on rather than buying. So its momentum is weak and when momentum is weak, we can't expect RSI to touch 70 levels on the upside and we should expect RSI to breech 30 line rather more frequently.

Let us see the weekly chart of Coal India, where range shift applies to a large extent. At the left hand on RSI panel, you can observe that it was above 70 (actually it was on 78), then during the downturn it fell down to below 20 levels. Then it turned up and reached 60 level, but couldn't touch 70 line. It tried to touch 70 again and again, but couldn't succeed. To be fair, it didn't fall to 20 levels also. So let us disallow this range shift rule in the Indian context.

Now look at the chart of Coal India (remember it is weekly).

- The top dotted line on RSI panel represents 70 level.
- The second top dotted line represents 60 level.
- And the dotted line at the bottom represents 30 level.

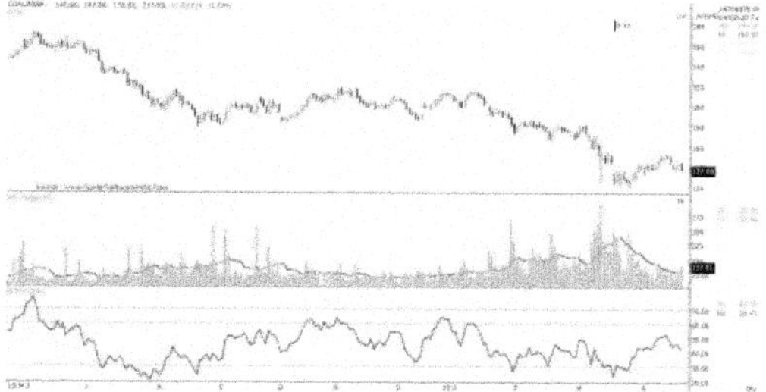

In the above chart, you can see that RSI was above 70 initially. Then it went below 30, recovered, but for the rest of the period, it could not reach above 60 level, indicating that now Coal India has turned bearish and it has shifted its normal trading range.

If RSI cannot push above the 60 level then there is weakness in the market.
If RSI cannot go down below the 40 level, then there is strength in the market.

If RSI retraces from 70 and remains above 50, it shows bullish trend. In fact, it indicates that it is making room for further bullish movement of price.

Likewise, if RSI rises from 30 and remains below 50, it shows bearish trend.

The range shift of RSI warns of potential trend changes. It predicts that the trend is going to change, as momentum has shifted.

The range shift gives us another significant clue. It tells that when RSI crosses its 60 levels on the upside, it starts a bullish rally and we should not expect this rally to end when RSI reaches 70 levels.

As per Paul Dean, anytime price is trending down the trader should be watching for Range Shifts up, and when price is trending up the trader should look for Range Shifts down. The shorter the time frame traded, the more often this will happen.

In the above statement of Paul Dean, perhaps the key to the mystery of range shift lies. This rule of range shift may be, just may be, applied to minute charts. But day traders needn't bother; this rule is not for you. This range shift rule is for short-term charts or rather minute-charts.

As I have already said in the beginning, a serious study about RSI in the Indian context has never been done, so we don't exactly know which theories work here and which don't. Now we have seen that the theory of range shift doesn't work in the Indian context, at least in the daily charts.

6. Channels & Trendlines

You can draw trendlines and channels on the RSI panel too, as you do on the price panel.

RSI trendlines can also be drawn to work as resistance and support lines. This way you would have a good idea of stock support and resistance levels. It may also help in profit booking also.

RSI gives trendline and channel breakouts too (I have discussed it at length in my previous Kindle book **'How to See a Breakout before It really happens: Breakout Signals in Descending Channels'**).

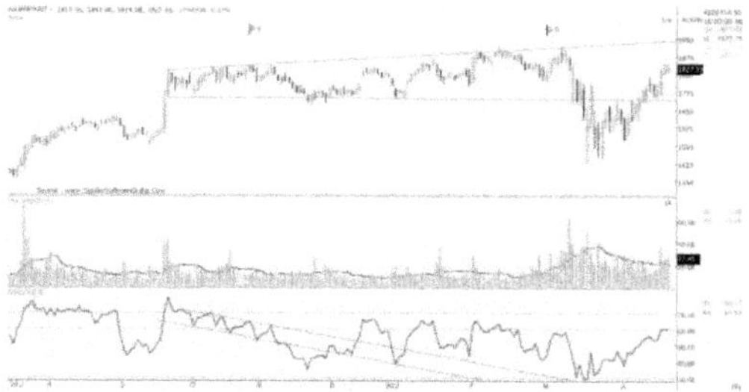

General rule of channels is that if a stock is running in a channel, you should draw an identical channel on RSI, so that you can compare the two channels and see deviations, if any.

However, RSI experts advise that we should make RSI channels in the opposite direction of the price trend (as you can see above). During down trends, draw ascending channels and during uptrends, draw descending channels. RSI has a limited moving space from 0-100, so it will have to move out of its channel and this channel shift can give you a signal about the bearishness or bullishness of the stock. Walter J. Baeyens in particular advises to use RSI channels to give buy and sell signals.

7. Chart patterns like Triangles, Head & Shoulders, Inverted H&S etc.

On the RSI panel, you can see several candlestick patterns like Head & Shoulders, pennants or triangles and you can trade them just like you do them on price chart. As Wilder puts it, 'The Index will display graphic chart formations which may not be obvious on a corresponding bar chart. For instance, head and shoulders, tops or bottoms, pennants or triangles often show up on the index to indicate breakouts and buy and sell points.' It means that RSI can predict breakouts well in advance.
Some of these patterns are, what Wilder calls chart formations:

- RSI makes higher highs, higher lows. This indicates that the momentum is rising and buy strength is more than sell strength. However, at some point it may stop doing it and will give either a divergence or a reversal signal.

- RSI makes lower highs, lower lows. This indicates that the momentum is slowing down and selling pressure is more than the buying pressure. However, at some point it may also signal either divergence or reversal.
- RSI makes Head & Shoulders pattern (Bearish) or Inverted Head & Shoulders pattern (Bullish). The concept and trading rules are the same as on price chart, however this pattern can be observed more frequently on RSI panel than on price panel, because H&S is valid only on peaks and Inverted H&S is valid only in valleys. Price doesn't make peaks and valleys so often than does RSI. So watch out for Head & Shoulders (around 70 levels) or its opposite Inverted Head & Shoulders pattern (around 30 levels) on RSI panel.

If you don't have an idea of what Head & Shoulders look like, see the picture given below.

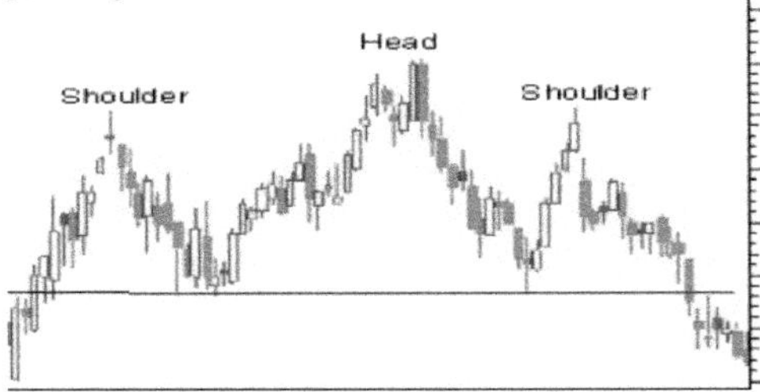

Inverted Head & Shoulders is just the opposite of Head & Shoulders, as you can see in the picture below.

- RSI makes double top or double bottom. RSI can make double tops at 70 levels or double bottoms at 30 levels to indicate trend reversals, even before they happen. And the beauty of it is that while making such patterns, RSI also gives a divergence. At double top it gives a bearish divergence, which indicates that bullish trend is over or at least on hold for some time. At double bottom it gives a bullish divergence, which indicates that bearish trend is over or at least it is time for some retracement.
- RSI makes triangles. RSI triangles are often centered around 50 level, indicating indecision about the future direction. At some point, the RSI breaks out of the triangle one way or the other and there is a swift move in both the RSI and price in the near future. And this is as it should be. When momentum shifts, price has to shift as well, as momentum is the power or fuel behind significant price move.

8. 9 day RSI Average Crossover

You can draw averages of RSI too. Usually 9 day Exponential Average is applied to RSI. When the RSI crosses its Average Line from below to above, it is considered a buy signal and vice versa.

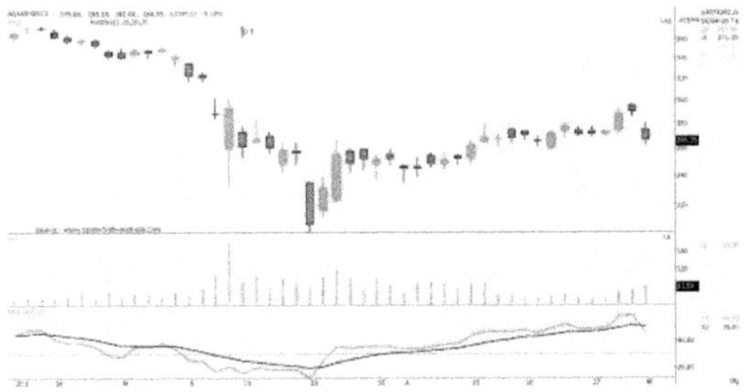

This average line is just an additional helping tool, as it compares current RSI level with its previous exponential 9 day average. However, this crossover should not be the basis of trading, as RSI can change track after giving a little breakout or breakdown. So it should be confirmed with other bullish or bearish signals or patterns.

Cardwell suggests using 9 period SMA (simple moving average) and 45 period WMA (Weighted moving average) of RSI to find out the short-term and intermediate trend. If the 9 period SMA is above 45 period WMA, it is bullish.

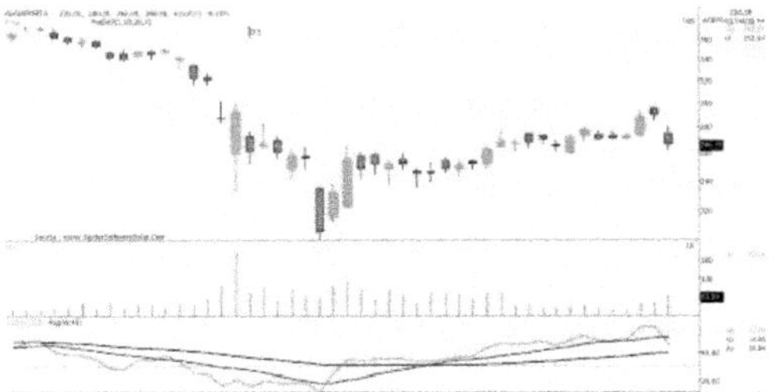

You can experiment here and enhance your learning.If you are drawing a moving average on price panel, do the same on RSI panel (the same moving average, like if you are drawing 20DMA on price panel, draw 20DMA on rsi panel also and check the result. This may tell you something more about price-RSI relation.

I am given an example of Adani Port chart, which we have been using in this section:

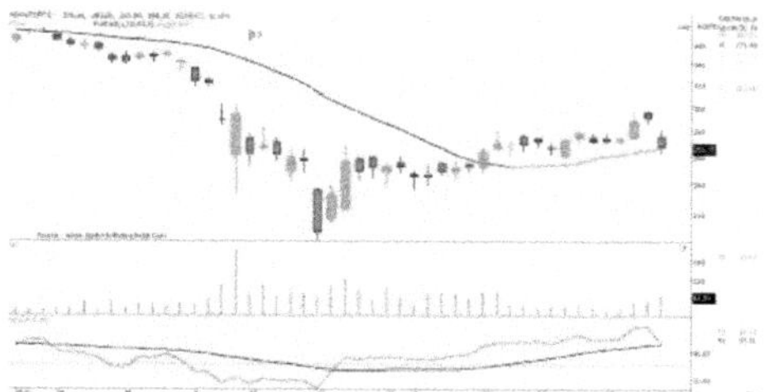

Now look, RSI MA signal came much earlier and it predicted the price movement well in advance. If you had waited for the moving average crossover on price panel, it would be lagging by 8-10 days. So always remember that RSI is a leading indicator and its moving averages can often predict price movements too.

9. Divergences: Bullish and Bearish (Will be discussed at length in **Chapter 5**)

10. Reversals: Positive and Negative (Will be discussed at length in **Chapter 6**)

So in this chapter we have learnt about the top 10 signals of RSI, or rather top 8 signals of RSI, as you have yet to go through divergences and reversals, which are considered to be the most powerful signals of RSI.

After reading the next two chapters, you will complete your RSI signal study and you can try them at your system. I don't know of any free software, on which you can draw moving average on RSI panel; I have done it on my SPIDER software.

However, if you can't find any free sotware, you can calculate Simple Moving Average (9) of RSI on your notebook any time. Note down the level of previous 9 days Smoothed RSI from ChartNexus (Remember, Smoothed RSI) .

Add them up and divide the total by 9; here is your 9 day SMA of RSI. It would be somewhat complicated, but don't forget that RSI inventor Wilder calculated the whole thing on sheets.

CHAPTER 5: DIVERGENCES: BULLISH & BEARISH

'Divergence is the single most indicative characteristic of the Relative Strength Index.' - J. Welles Wilder

- **What is a divergence?**
- **Theory 1: Divergences are very powerful signals**
- **Theory 2: Divergences are minor signals**
- **Wait for multiple divergences!**
- **Duration is important**
- **Confirm the validity by price action**
- **Confirm the validity by candlesticks**
- **Confirm the validity by volume**

As Wilder puts it, 'Divergence between price action and the RSI is a very strong indicator of a market turning point. Divergence occurs when the RSI is increasing and the price movement is either flat or decreasing. Conversely, divergence occurs when the RSI is decreasing and price movement is either flat or increasing.'

What is a Divergence?

Divergence means non-confirmation. Price is moving in a way, which is not supported by RSI.

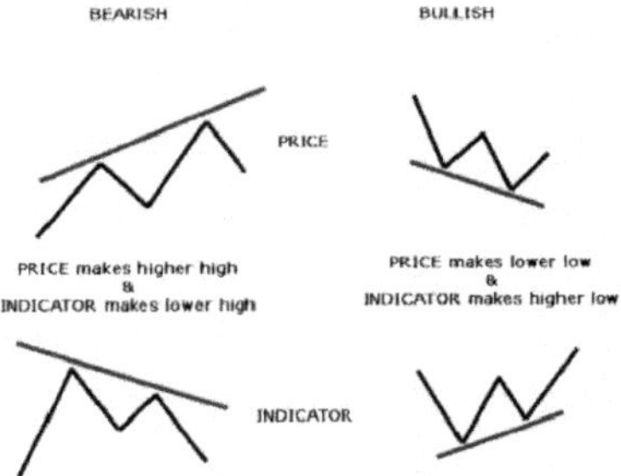

As you can observe in the above picture,

- Bearish divergence occurs, when price makes higher high and RSI makes lower high.
- Bullish divergence occurs, when price makes lower low and RSI makes higher low.

Usually divergences are to be found at the extreme end of the RSI scale. Bearish divergences are to be found around 70 levels and bullish divergences are to be found around 30 level.

There is a positive divergence if the price chart still shows lower bottoms while the opposite occurs in the RSI chart line. This is a sign that the strength and momentum of the falling price movement is decreasing - at least temporarily - and thus increasing the likelihood of an interim price upturn.

Bullish Divergence	Made at the bottom, made in bearish trend, bullish signal	Price makes new lows, RSI makes higher lows
Bearish Divergence	Made at the top, made in bullish trend, bearish signal	Price makes new highs, RSI makes lower lows

To make it easy for you, I would reproduce the pictures, which you have already seen in the calculation section.

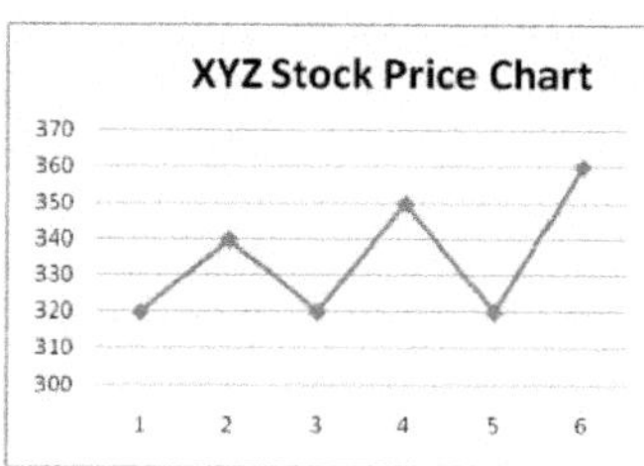

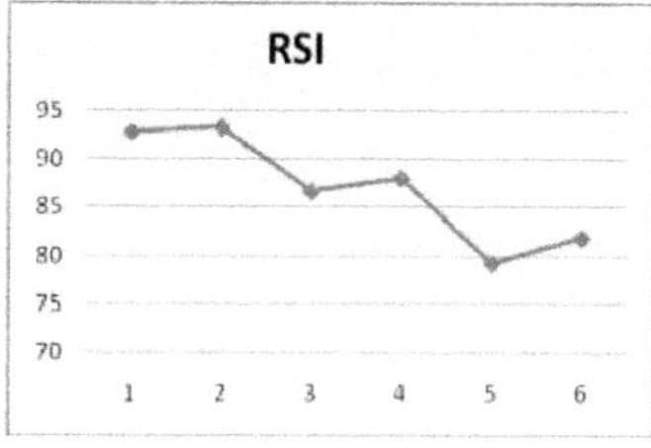

Theory 1: Divergences are Very Powerful Signals

RSI divergence is a signal that RSI has reached overbought/oversold levels and it is also a signal that the momentum is changing and the current trend is weakening.

Divergence is one of the most powerful signals of RSI. Due to its anti-trend bias, RSI alerts traders about the possibility of trend reversal or at least retracement.

As Paul Dean observes, 'Divergences act like little spies alerting you to events before they happen so that you will have an edge.'

Also remember that RSI divergence is not a common signal, which can be seen or appreciated by all the technical analysts. It is usually not generated accurately enough by computer softwares, so most of the traders fail to notice it.

According to Wilder, the inventor of RSI, divergence is the most significant predictive feature of RSI.

On the other hand, according to Cardwell school, divergences don't mean reversals; they only signify retracement or correction.

You are free to choose your side, however I would stick to the side of the inventor.

Divergences can be very good clues to tell us what is coming and what to expect. In most of the cases divergences may be telling us the truth about the direction of the market or stock, but in a few cases they may fail.

Note: In my study of RSI divergences, I have found that they are frequently successful, but only when they are found at the top or bottom of the price panel. If you observe RSI divergence in the middle of the panel, it may not be a powerful signal. That means, for trend reversal firstly it is necessary to have a solid and powerful trend. The stronger the trend, the more powerful RSI divergence signal would be.

Divergences have meaning only at top/bottom of price panel; they don't mean much during consolidation period, as they are not found on the top or bottom of the price panel, but in between. In my study, I have found that in such cases RSI divergence didn't immediately give results.

Theory 2: Divergences are Minor Signals

Cardwell says, 'Both Bullish and Bearish Divergence usually cause a brief price correction and not an actual trend reversal.'

According to him, divergence is a minor signal. He demotes the brainchild of his teacher Wilder to promote his own brainchild: Reversals. Cardwell says that positive and negative reversals are powerful signals, as these are the dynamites, true power of RSI.

Cardwell school's opinion is that Price/RSI divergence is not an exceptional signal. It occurs frequently, as it is inevitable and does not warrant any special treatment. It is just one way for the RSI to escape its mathematical constraints (remember our anti-trend discussion from Chapter 3: Real Secret is in its Calculation Method).

John Hayden makes fun of divergences by saying, 'Going long when a bullish divergence makes its appearance is a certain way to make small profits and generate large losses.'

But not in our study! Our study shows that divergences work. However, it should be kept it in mind that it often takes multiple divergences, before the trend reverses.

Walter J. Baeyens also belittles divergences and says, 'Divergence occurs frequently and it does not have any special significance.'

In my opinion, Walter J. Baeyens misses the point completely. Divergences don't, in fact they can't, occur every fortnight, as trends don't change so fast. A real trend can go on for several months or years, for that matter.

Perhaps Baeyens is not talking about extreme divergences here, when price is at the top or bottom. He seems to talk about minor divergences, when RSI reaches 70 or 30 levels (which happens more frequently).

Cardwell noted that bearish divergence: 1) only occurs in uptrends, and 2) mostly only leads to a brief correction instead of a reversal in trend. Therefore, bearish divergence is a sign confirming an uptrend.

Similarly, according to Cardwell, bullish divergence is a sign confirming a downtrend. Of course, Cardwell was equating bullish divergence with negative reversal and bearish divergence with positive reversal.

What Cardwell doesn't realise that price/RSI divergences may be common, but the divergence about which Wilder is talking is very uncommon and is seen infrequently.

Real Divergences are few and far between, whereas reversals are more common. Trends don't change every month in stock market, however positive or negative reversals can occur every month.

Cardwell's or rather Cardwell school's problem with RSI divergence is simple: in RSI divergence, You can't determine entry point, exit point, stop loss or target of price objective. Divergence is not an exact trading tool in itself, this is why Cardwell or other traders don't consider it significant.

As Paul Dean sums it up, 'A divergence although tempting to trade does not give you any target so it is impossible to determine your Risk Reward Ratio.'

Wait for Multiple Divergences!

I have found in my study that RSI can give more than one divergence, and frequently does so. This is why don't rush in to buy after seeing the first divergence. My observation is that RSI gives at least two divergence signals and only then the trend reverses. However, three RSI divergences in close succession are enough to change the direction of the price.

Important Tip : Don't expect that market will immediately reverse after a RSI divergence. Trend has to slow down first, then stop and then reverse. All this takes time.

Now I am showing you a chart, where price retraced after the first divergence, but the trend didn't reverse and the stock made another new low, giving second divergence. This will warn you that you shouldn't rush in to buy, as soon as you see a divergence. Because multiple divergences may come.

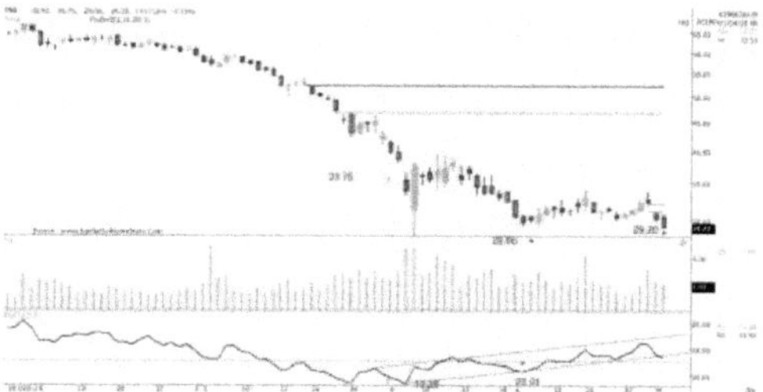

Above we see the daily chart of PNB, which made a bottom on price as well as RSI, when price was at 33.75.

Then the price kept on going lower and made a new low at 29.65. However, RSI didn't make another low, but was higher than point 1, so there was Bullish divergence.

Remember, here RSI has made an ascending channel, which it finally breaks when it makes a fresh new low of 29.20 (and no need to tell you that RSI is higher than point 2, so there was Bullish Divergence No. 2 (You can't see the green candle, which came after divergence point 2).

Duration is Important

This is a reminder that unless you find a divergence in close-by candles, price reversal may need multiple divergences. Far-off divergences are apt to fail, as they tell two different momentum stories. This is why close-by divergence points are considered more powerful.

As John Hayden points out, 'The duration of a divergence is important. A two to six day divergence usually indicates that a detour in price is more likely than a longer period. A longer divergence period of weeks and even months, if using daily charts, is usually less indicative that a price detour is coming. The most powerful divergence occurs during a 2 or 3 period divergence.'

According to Cardwell, number of periods between point 1 and point 2 of divergence are important. Those divergences are more powerful and strong, which come within 2-6 periods, whereas divergences found in more than 6 periods are not that significant. This is certainly correct. The nearest the divergence candles, the more powerful the signal and the swifter the price reaction.

See the above chart of Nifty (Feb-Mar 2020). Here Nifty is falling down sharply. Price makes a new low (observe the first vertical line from the left on RSI panel). RSI also makes a new low. Price falls some more and makes another, but RSI doesn't make another low and makes a higher low (observe the second verticla line in the middle of the RSI panel). Then after a green candle, price makes another lower low. As you can clearly see in the third vertical line from the left, RSI doesn't make a lower low, but makes a higher low. And soon after, price reverses. It took two divergences to make it happen.

RSI divergence signals are useful for those who focus primarily on counter-trend strategies. They enable investors to identify changes in trends at a very early stage. However, it remains important to realize that in many cases the counter-reaction to the existing trend will be short-lived and instead of trend-reversal, it may end up as a retracement or correction. That is why they are perhaps better suited to those who like to act a little more aggressively in the very short term.

Confirm the Validity by Price Action

If you want to be very sure about a divergence, don't do anything initially. Let the price action confirm RSI signals.

Suppose you see a bearish divergence on the chart. You just wait for the price to make a lower low. If the price keeps on making higher lows, consider that RSI signal has become nullified.

In my studies, price often makes higher high and throws up another RSI divergence. Here also try to confirm the signal.

Rule of Thumb : When divergences come, they come in a pair of three, or at least two.

When the price makes a lower low, the RSI signal of bearish divergence would be confirmed. This is exactly the concept of Failure Swing, which we have already discussed in the chapter, 'The Top 10 Signals of RSI .'

- In the case of bearish divergence, wait for the price to make a lower low (as it has already made a lower high in the process of giving divergence).
- In the case of bullish divergence, wait for the price to make a higher high (as it has made a higher low in the process of giving divergence).

Remember, whether it is a bearish divergence or bullish divergence, it needs to be confirmed by price action. If the time interval between the diverging candles is less, price would quickly change its course and follow RSI.

Of course, it may reduce your profit potential to some extent and you will miss most of the opportunity.

Confirm the Validity by Candlesticks

This is not for conservative traders, but rather for aggressive traders: confirmation by Candlestick patterns.

Candlestick patterns or a single candle can also confirm trend reversals.

The following are the most common trend reversal signals found in a candlestick chart:

- **Morning Star (bullish) and Evening Star (bearish)**
- **Abandoned Baby**
- **Doji Star**
- **Spinning Top**
- **Hammer**
- **Bullish Engulfing and Bearish Engulfing**

If you find them soon after the divergence signal, most probably the divergence is valid.

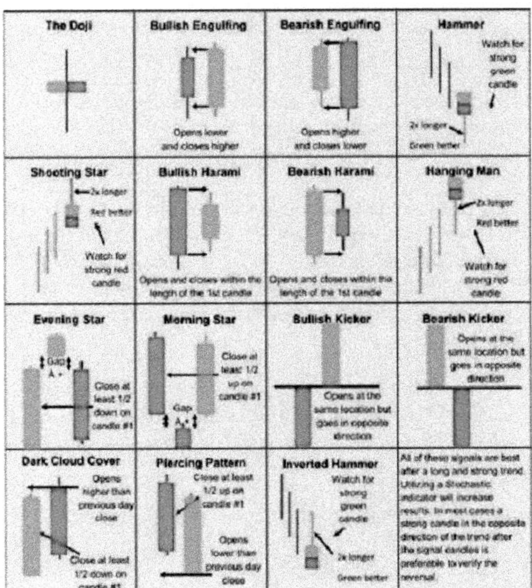

Confirm the Validity by Volume

Volume shift may also confirm the divergence. In the downtrend, price was falling down on high volume. But after divergence, the volume dries up, because now the price movement is against the trend, for the time being. If the volume dries up, it is a signal that traders are cautious and not entering the new trend, but waiting for confirmation.

If the volume picks up and you observe higher volume on those candles which are in the direction of new trend, it confirms the validity of the divergence.

Example of Bearish Divergence in close-by candles: HUL

I have retrieved an old chart of bearish divergence from files. Here divergence takes place on Oct. 23, 2014, Deepavali Muhurat trading chart.

As you can see, it is a very powerful divergence, with a signal count of 3 (that means, divergence took place on the third day after the initial top/bottom). If you remember our discussion of chapter 3 , you know that 3 candles are minimum for a divergence.

- First bullish, second bearish, third bullish (in a bearish divergence).
- First bearish, second bullish, third bearish (in a bullish divergence).

Thereafter the stock market was closed from Oct. 24-26 due to weekend and holidays.

Below you can see the chart of the next day (it is a daily chart, but still you will get a rough idea of how quickly divergence gave its results).

HUL fell 5% on flat results (the second last candle is of Oct. 27 on daily chart).

Here we get the idea that RSI signals of smaller timeframe can also give good results in higher timeframes.

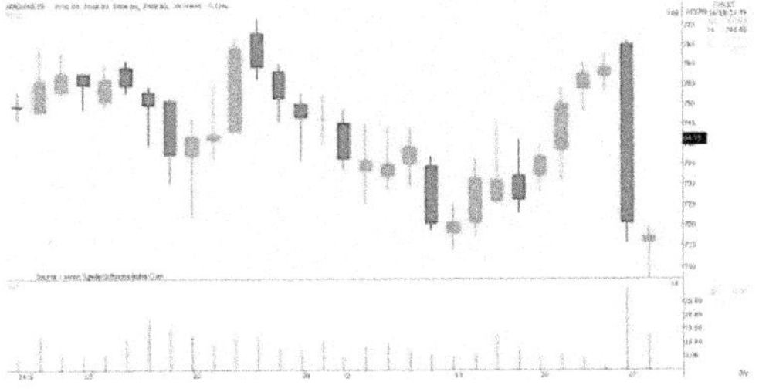

Example of Bearish Divergence in Far-Off Candles: Nifty 60 minutes

CHAPTER 6: REVERSALS: POSITIVE & NEGATIVE

'If you pick up only a single notion from this book. let it be the following: When an oscillator advances or declines disproportionately to the markets' movement, you are on the wrong side of the market if you are positioned with the oscillator.' - Constance Brown

- Key differences between divergences and reversals
- Positive Reversals & Negative Reversals
- Positive Reversals
- Negative Reversals
- How to calculate price target?
- Price target formula of a positive reversal signal
- Price target formula of a negative reversal signal
- Confirmation of reversals
- Reversals are trend continuation signals
- Close-by reference points are more powerful

As I have already told you, Positive and Negative Reversals were not invented by Welles Wilder, but are Andrew Cardwell's contribution to RSI.

Welles Wilder moved on to other things, but Cardwell stuck with RSI and in doing so discovered reversals. Some people also name them 'hidden divergences,' which is a highly confusing term and adds complexity to an already complex RSI world.

Key Differences Between Divergences and Reversals

Remember, reversals are different from divergences; in fact, they are just the opposite.

	Divergences	**Reversals**
Trend	Divergences signify trend reversals.	Reversals signify trend continuation
Measurement during downtrend	Divergence is measured off of the lows of *price and the indicator* during a downtrend.	Negative Reversal is measured off of the highs of *price and the indicator* during a downtrend
Measurement during uptrend	Divergence is measured off of the highs of *price and the indicator* during an uptrend.	Positive Reversal is measured off of the lows of *price and the indicator* during an uptrend.
Placement	At the extreme range of the price chart AND near overbought/oversold levels of RSI	Reversals are found mostly in mid-range of the panel

- Trendline for positive reversals is drawn at bottom/support line of price and RSI charts (Just like we do in bullish divergence).
- Trendline for negative reversals is drawn at top/resistance line of price and RSI charts (Just like we do in bearish divergence).

	uptrend	downtrend
Retracement pattern	occurs in uptrend retracements	occurs in downtrend retracements
Price/RSI lows	Price makes higher lows, RSI makes lower lows	Price makes lower highs, RSI makes higher highs
Measurement	measured off of the lows of price and indicator	measured off of the highs of price and indicator
Placement	in the middle of price chart	in the middle of price chart

Positive Reversals

Positive reversals are seen during uptrends. They occur at the time of corrections or retracements, when stock falls due to normal profit booking of traders and not due to serious sell-off.

As the stock is running in a strong uptrend, its Up Average for the past 14 days is significantly high. When there is a reverse movement in price, RSI reacts strongly and falls disproportionately.

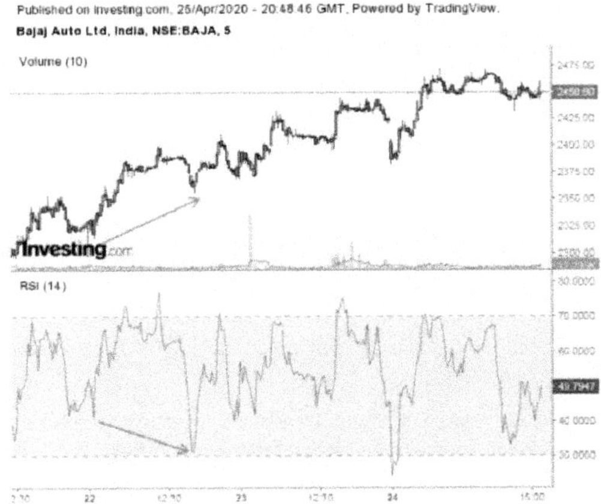

As we have seen in our discussion in **Chapter 3: Real Secret of RSI is in Its Calculation Method** , RSI moves disproportionately on anti-trend prices. So RSI falls down more than it should and in this process creates a positive reversal.

After retracement, new buyers come in and even those join in who have booked profit, as they once again find the stock price attractive. The momentum builds up and the uptrend continues.

Negative Reversals

Negative reversals come during downtrends. Stock is falling down and RSI is also falling down with it.

Suddenly short-sellers book profit and there is short covering. Price moves up slightly, but RSI moves up sharply on this anti-trend price action.

And in this process it creates a negative reversal.

After retracement, new short-sellers join or the old short-sellers rejoin the party and due to this the downtrend continues.

Important Tip : Spike lows of RSI are observed in an uptrend and spike highs of RSI are observed in a downtrend.

How to Calculate Price Target?

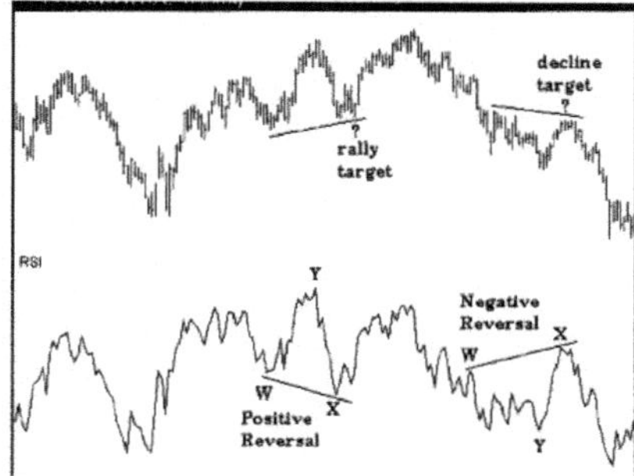

Positive and Negative reversals are preferred by traders, as here you can set targets and stop losses, which is difficult in the case of divergence. Here you know where to enter and where to place your stop loss.

Good traders want to determine Reward to Risk Ratio in advance. And to know this ratio, they have to know their entry price, stop loss and target price.

Price Target Formula of a Positive Reversal Signal

Price Target = (X-W)+Y

Note: Don't get confused that X is lower than W (I know this, as I was confused at first also). You are looking at the wrong panel. See the price panel, where price at X is higher than price at W. So the formula is all right. You just have to find what the price was at W, X and Y of RSI.

Suppose price at W point was 100 and price at X was 110 and Price at Y was 130. Now we put these numbers in our formula to calculate our projected price target:

Projected price target = (X-W)+Y

(110-100)+130

=140

So the price target is 140.

We can enter at 115 with a stop loss at 109 (below the recent low of 110).

If we do so, here is our trade setup:

Risk = Rs. 7

Reward = Rs. 25

Reward to Risk Ratio = 25:7

= 3.6:1

Not bad!

Price Target Formula of a Negative Reversal Signal

Suppose in a negative reversal, price at W point was 110 and price at X was 100 and Price at Y was 80. Now we put these numbers in our formula to calculate our projected price target:

Projected price target = Y-(W-X)

= 80 - (110-100)

= 70

So the projected price target is 70.

Here also you can determine your stop loss, may be at 101, one rupee more than X.

And then it is easy to calculate your Reward to Risk ratio.

Suppose you enter at 95 (this much margin has to be left, because pattern recognition takes time, there are ask-bid spreads and there are commissions, brokerage etc. too).

Entry = 95

Target price = 70

Stop loss = 101

Reward Risk ratio = 25:6

=4.2:1

What are you waiting for? Go, shortsell it.

Confirmation of Reversals

Cardwell advised that we should not buy or sell on seeing reversals. Rather, we should confirm the signal, whether it is valid or not.

His recommendation is to get confirmation from the moving averages of RSI (not of Price).

- Confirmation of Positive reversal - 9SMA & WMA of RSI should point upwards.
- Confirmation of Negative reversal - 9SMA & 45 WMA of RSI should point downwards.

Cancellation: If divergence trendline is broken, it cancels out the divergence.

When you get opposite signal, you book profit and exit. As Paul Dean says, 'The Positive Reversal is over as soon as the NR is confirmed.

What do we do? Exit. Simple.'

Reversals are Trend Continuation Signals

Reversal patterns are primarily useful for trend traders, as the occurence of this pattern signals that prices have made a corrective retracement in a larger trend -- and that the trend is ready to resume.

The main benefit of trading with reversal pattern is that the majority of the market's momentum is on your side, as you are trading in the same direction as the larger trend.

This is a key difference between the reversal pattern and the classic divergence, and one that many new traders miss when looking to implement these strategies. The occurrence of a reversal pattern can also act as a confirmation that the original trend is still valid.

Close-by Reference Points are More Powerful

Cardwell prefers close reference points for his reversal patterns. That means that they should ideally be separated by a single price bar. Such signals are 'strong' signals, which are separated by one or two bars, as they ensure that projected targets are achieved.

For example, let us talk about positive reversals. A stock makes a low at 85 (W), next day it gives a green candle at 90 (Y), on the third day it makes a red candle at 88(X). What would be the projected target:

Remember the formula for positive reversals:

Projected price target = (X-W)+Y

= (88-85)+90

=93

Can you see the problem here?

Try putting stoploss and try to calculate the Reward to Risk Ratio.

Now perhaps you might see the problem: Profit margin is too low.

So why did Cardwell advocate it so strongly?

The key is in the details.

Perhaps Cardwell laid down this rule for Forex markets, where low profit margins are considered the norm.

But the real reason is this. We are thinking in terms of daily charts, but Cardwell preferred weekly charts and we all know that a weekly candle is necessarily bigger.

Cardwell's insistence on close reference points can only be understood in terms of weekly or monthly chart.

On a weekly chart, a stock makes a low at 85 (W), next day it gives a green candle at 125 (Y), on the third day it makes a red candle at 90(X). What would be the projected target:

Projected price target = (X-W)+Y

= (90-85)+125

=130

Now the Reward to Risk Ratio, stoploss and projected price target all fall in line.

So here we conclude our discussion of The Top 10 Signals of RSI , which we started in Chapter 4 .

In the next chapter, we would look at the limitations of RSI. It can create magic, yet it does not mean that it can create magic all the time, at all places, in all markets and in all stocks.

Up to now we have learnt when we should use RSI; now we will learn when not to use RSI.

CHAPTER 7: LIMITATIONS OF RSI

'Markets tend to operate in a trading range 70-75% of the time and trend 25-30% of the time. Consequently, any moving average time period should be equally effective in a trending market and no moving average is effective in a trading range market. Conversely, oscillators that identify areas of overbought and oversold are most effective in trading range or sideways markets.' - Thomas DeMark

RSI is a dynamic indicator, which goes beyond its functions as a momentum oscillator. However, like any other indicator, it has its own limitations.

You have to be aware of these limitations, so that you don't use it where RSI can't be or shouldn't be used.

- First of all, RSI is a momentum oscillator, so it does not work well in trends, or so people say. This is the general consensus about RSI. However, as we have seen divergences and reversals can work well during trends also. So this limitation is not 100% correct.
- It does not work well in illiquid or low-float scrips, so don't try to trade low-float or low-volume stocks on the basis of RSI. And the reason is simple: small quantity buy or sell can swing prices disproportionately. Look for a stock with good volume, preferably above 1 lakh shares daily.
- It does not work well in operator-driven stocks or circuit stocks.
- It does not work properly in a stock with very high volatility and in such cases RSI may give inconsistent signals.
- Theoretically it does not work well in index charts, though it works like

a charm in Nifty chart. Theory is that an index is a sum of several stocks, so the cumulative movement may not give consistent readings. However, practically I have seen it working well on Nifty 50 index.

- It is calculated only on the basis of closing prices, so day highs or day lows will not be counted, even if such price movements are significant.
- It may give false or disproportionate signals, especially in anti-trend direction. A small anti-trend price action may cause major movement in RSI.
- As we have already discussed in Chapter 1 , RSI on various sites give different readings, so ensure its correct reading. For the purposes of this book, always consult RSI at free online charting website investing.com.
- Day traders prefer to use short periods on RSI; some use even 3 or 2 period RSI to generate more signals.
- Use of RSI is very subjective. Trader's experience plays a crucial role.
- In a nutshell, RSI gives us the snapshot of bear-bull power balance. Whenever there is momentum shift due to some significant news, RSI alerts us about it before price action. It is very sensitive to any changes in momentum. Other indicators need signal lines or support of multiple moving averages, but a single RSI line is capable of doing all this work and even better than them.
- If anybody tells you trading is simple, don't believe him at all. He is kidding or he has the mentality of a kid. Stock market is full of jolly-hearted professionals, whose mission in life is to make the life of retail traders difficult and teach them some lessons in the bargain. They use shakeouts and fakeouts with RSI too, just like your centre forward does in hockey: feigning to do one thing, while actually planning to do another thing.
- The most popular feigning trick is that when the professionals want to give a breakout, they just pause the buying pressure. RSI is very volatile around 70, so even with slight decrease it comes below 70, by which retail traders think that RSI is reversing and now the price is going to fall down; so some of them sell or even short sell the stock. Then the laughing professionals put the pressure on the buy pedal and kill the short-sellers by staging a breakout.

CHAPTER 8: WHICH TIMEFRAME IS BEST?

'Well, I use 14-period on a monthly, weekly, daily, hourly, 15-minute chart, 5-minute chart. The rules don't change depending on the temperament and investment objective of a trader.' -Andrew Cardwell

- **Challenge of deciding chart timeframe**
- **Which timeframe is best?**
- **One level up, one level down**
- **Challenge of deciding the number of periods in RSI**
- **Challenge of deciding the trend**
- **Why timeframe is important?**
- **Challenge of multiple overbought/oversold levels**

There are so many timeframes that you get different RSI signals regarding buy, sell or hold. (I wonder, if anyone got a RSI signal of HOLD!)

In Chapter 1 , we had talked about several challenges in RSI trading; one of the major challenges is regarding timeframe.

Challenge of Deciding Chart Timeframe

Look at the various timeframe chart options available on Investing.com

1. 1 min chart
2. 5 min chart
3. 15 min chart
4. 30 min chart
5. 45 min chart
6. 1 hour chart
7. 2 hour chart
8. 4 hour chart
9. 5 hour chart
10. 1 day chart
11. 1 week chart
12. 1 month chart

Interesting note: Spide Software provides a still higher time frame chart option: 3 month chart (Quarterly chart).

When there are 12 timeframe charts, naturally there would be 12 different RSI levels of a single stock or index at any point of time.

I will show you an example after the market close on 5.5.2020

Timeframe	**RSI level**
1 min chart	56.25
5 min chart	30.23
15 min chart	32.12
30 min chart	28.35
45 min chart	33.10

1 hour chart	34.56
2 hour chart	41.72
4 hour chart	48.15
5 hour chart	48.08
1 day chart	48.51
1 week chart	36.89
1 month chart	39.53
Average RSI	39.79

Now let us briefly discuss what the different RSI levels tell us.

- 1 min chart has the highest reading of RSI. It means that in the last 14 minutes, buy momentum was stronger than sell momentum. Other minute charts are showing lesser RSI readings, so we may conclude that it was a down day and so the 1 min chart is showing short covering and intraday settlement or profit booking.
- Five of these charts from 5 min chart to 1 hour chart show RSI around 30 level. It means that there RSI is near oversold levels and current trend is likely to be down. Minute charts low readings also tell that it was a down day.
- Three of these charts (4 hour, 5 hour and 1 day) are showing RSI around 48 levels; it means that buy and sell equation is almost in equilibrium. It indicates that over the past two weeks, momentum has been uncertain and there may be some indecision about the direction.

Interesting Note: By the way, do you know anybody, who trades on the basis of 2 hour or 4 hour chart or 5 hour chart? I didn't even know they existed.

Weekly RSI is at 37 and monthly RSI is at 39.

Weekly RSI is less than the daily RSI, which means that market has crashed within previous 14 weeks.

Which Timeframe is Best?

Remember, price levels remain unchanged in all time frames, but RSI levels change in different time frames. And this is the root of a lot of confusion.

Why?

Because RSI is calculated on the closing price of a bar. In 1 min chart, RSI changes every minute because price makes a new candle every minute and RSI is calculated every minute. In 1 day chart, it changes every day because price makes a new candle every day. So RSI in different time frames keeps giving different readings.

These different time frames pose a unique challenge for traders: Which timeframe is best?

Well it depends! It depends on your psychology, your capital, your holding capacity, your profit expectations and whether you have the luxury of sitting in front of your computer during market hours for day-trading. If you trade only on a part-time basis and you have some other full-time job or profession, obviously day-trading is not a viable option for you. So you can conveniently forget minute charts.

Though there are several opinions regarding it, the overall consensus is this:

- For day trading: 5 minute chart, 15 minute chart
- For swing/positional trading: 1 hour chart
- For short term trading (less than a year): Daily chart
- For Long term trading (more than a year): Weekly chart

One Level Up, One Level Down

Always consult the charts of one level up and one level down.

What does it mean? It means that if you are trading on the basis of daily chart, you should also look at one level up (in this case, weekly) and one level down (1 hour chart) to filter the noise and get proper perspective.

Focus: Daily chart

One-level up: Weekly chart

One-level down: 1 hour chart.

You may ask, for one-level down why we shouldn't choose 5-hour chart? Your query is valid, but the answer is obvious. Theoretically speaking, 5 hour chart is the next timeframe, but virtually nobody trades on the basis of 2 hour, 4 hour or 5 hour charts. So the next logical down level is 1 hour chart.

Most of the traders use 1 minute, 5 minute, 15 minute, 1 hour, 1 day, 1 week charts only. So though theoretically there are 12 timeframes available on Investing.com, practically there are only 6 time frames to choose from.

- 1 min chart
- 5 min chart
- 15 min chart
- 1 hour chart
- 1 day chart
- 1 week chart

If you follow this strategy of one level up and one level down, you will be better off. This gives you the advantage of seeing the price action through various viewpoints. It may also alert you to some red flag, which might be present in the lower or higher timeframe, but not present in your timeframe.

Remember the one step up and one step down formula and consult the charts of one step higher and one step lower time frame.

What is the advantage of consulting lower time frame charts? You will get to see earlier signals. A potential trend reversal is seen first in smaller time frames.

What is the advantage of consulting higher time frame charts? You will get to see the context or background. You will also get the idea of broader trend of your stock or index.

Some people say that RSI was invented for daily charts, so RSI works best in that timeframe.

However, Andrew Cardwell has shown that it can work equally well in the weekly timeframe also. But let us not forget that Cardwell had modified RSI to suit his purposes. If we want to trade a different timeframe other than daily, we can also do so. Remember, lower timeframe chart signals would give less profit percentage compared to higher timeframes. So don't expect to find a 20% profit projection signal on a 1 min chart. Be realistic and expect only a 2% profit signal on 1 min chart.

If you want a higher profit percentage, trade on the basis of higher timeframe charts. Though there is a catch: higher timeframes promise better profit, the drawback is that you will have to wait more to collect your profit. The more profit percentage you require, the higher timeframe you should choose, but also be ready to wait for a longer time to book it.

Challenge of Deciding the Number of Periods in RSI

Most day traders reduce the number of periods (n) on RSI to generate more signals. Reducing the number of periods makes the RSI more volatile (where you get more signals) and increasing the number of periods makes the RSI more stable (where you get less signals). Some day traders use 9 period RSI and some of them use even 3 or 2 period RSI.

However, there are some experts who strongly advise that a 14 period should always be used for RSI in all time horizons due to its peculiar predictive capacity. They say that only a 14 period RSI works effectively as a leading indicator. In other timeframes it somehow and somewhat loses its predictive power.

Challenge of Deciding the Trend

Let us not forget that when we shift our timeframe, the trend also shifts.

When you are looking at different timeframe charts, you should know what is the dominant trend in them. It is quite possible to find an uptrend in weekly chart and a downtrend in the daily chart and an uptrend in the hourly chart.

Now what to do? Which trend should you go with?

Deciding the trend is a crucial question for traders, as major price action happens with the trend, so it is said, 'trend is your friend.'

You simply write down:

Weekly : Up

Daily : Down

Hourly : Up

Of course, the higher timeframe chart determines the long term trend of the stock, but other timeframes play their role in determining intermediate and short-term trends.

In our example, weekly chart is in a primary uptrend. But its short-term trend is down. May be due to profit booking or retracement or newsflow or whatever. This is why you are observing down trend in the daily chart.

You should do well to remember that the daily chart is in downtrend, because a retracement is taking place in the weekly chart.

As soon as the weekly chart's retracement is over, you would see a shift in the daily chart trend and it will start a new uptrend. Perhaps around this time you would see a bullish divergence on daily chart, which would alert you that the trend is going to change. It will foretell that now daily chart is going to move in sync with the weekly chart's primary trend.

Larger timeframe charts determine long term trends, while shorter timeframe charts often give early signals about trend changes.

In a nutshell, this sums up the whole thing:

Timeframe	Primary Trend	Secondary Trend
Weekly Chart	Up	Down
Daily Chart	Down	Up
Hourly Chart	Up	

So you see, the secondary trend of the higher timeframe may become the primary trend of the lower timeframe.

Always get some clarity on trends in different timeframes, as it will save you a lot of confusion. When you look at three different timeframe charts, you may see conflicting signals on them. You may see a sell signal on daily chart, but a buy signal on hourly chart.

Usually we should trade in the direction of the one-step higher timeframe, so we can do one of these two things:

- Wait for those signals, which are in sync with the higher timeframe trend
- Enter anyway with tight stoploss

Why Timeframe is Important?

Choosing the right timeframe is important, because traders of every timeframe have distinct personalities.

If you trade a 5 min chart, you will think like those traders, who also trade on the basis of 5 min charts.

You won't care for long term approach, you will adhere to tight stop loss, you will look out for pennies and you will book profit quickly. Their motto is: quickly in, quickly out. They usually don't have much money or patience.

Nothing wrong in it! However, this is the typical personality of this particular timeframe and if you are trading on the basis of 5 min chart, you have to adopt this philosophy. A 5 min chart trader is not bothered about long-term profits or losses; he is not bothered whether a company is going to go bankrupt tomorrow. He is concerned only with here and now. This is why he will often take more risky trades.

Minute chart traders usually trade Future & Options, as they have better profit potential there. They lack a solid capital base, so they frequently trade on margins. You see, if you don't have much capital, you can't buy and hold stocks. You have to necessarily trade in the F&O segment. However, don't forget that even big institutions, FIIs and DIIs trade in F&O segment, who have a lot of capital at their disposal. For any retail trader, getting profits in F&O is like the David-Goliath fight.

On the other hand, typical daily chart traders are usually retail investors, who are working full time in some job or profession and they are investing their residual or disposable income with a trading time frame of months. Some of them can't track the market during market hours. They are not in a hurry to book profits and they have more money than day traders. They don't consult minute charts and they are not bothered about the short-term hiccups. They want higher profit percentage than day traders. Some of them are swing traders, some of them are SIP investors; most of them are part-time traders, who are investing their hard-earned money in stock market to earn a better yield than a bank FD. They are conservative and safety-oriented.

Those who trade on the basis of weekly chart are in a different class. Usually the opinion of the larger timeframe traders prevails, as they have more money, more patience and more power to move the markets for a longer period. Usually large timeframe investors are mutual funds, pension funds, big financial institutions, FIIs or big traders/investors. They typically have a longer timeframe and for short term profits, they trade in F&O segment. Remember, they are the experts with top degrees in Finance. And due to their clout, they often have access to insider news much earlier than retail traders.

Important tip : Daily charts are mostly used by the retail investors and weekly charts are mostly used by the institutional investors (though they sometimes pay attention to monthly charts also, as they invest for a longer period).

No wonder, retail shareholders and professionals don't seem to be at the same page! You see, they take decisions on the basis of different charts. So if you intend to trade like a pro, start paying attention to those charts which professionals see. In particular, study weekly charts well, as it is the favourite time-frame of big investors.

Challenge of Multiple Overbought/Oversold levels

Different timeframes can create some confusion in case of RSI.

Suppose you are a trader whose primary chart is daily chart.

You check one level down chart and in the 1 hour chart you find that RSI is above 70, which means overbought. You think instantly, is it going to fall from here?

You check the daily chart; there you find that RSI is at 60 levels and has plenty of space to move up.

And if you go one level up and check the weekly chart, you find that RSI is at 50 levels in weekly chart, so it is practically starting its upmove after crossing centreline.

Higher timeframe signals will prevail, but RSI will find a way to manage the whole thing. You see, in a strong uptrend, even a single red candle would bring the 1 hour RSI from 70 to 30 levels. Have faith in RSI and whenever you see overbought levels in a lower timeframe chart, be prepared to see a short period correction.

Important tip : If weekly trend is up and daily trend shows signs of weakness, it may be time of retracement in the weekly trend. So you can improve your timing if you use a lower time-frame chart to tell you the retracements of the higher time-frame.

CHAPTER 9: 20 POPULAR RSI TRADING STRATEGIES

'At best you may achieve a 60% win rate with any strategy, including one with the RSI.' -Tradingsim.com

1. RSI + Support/Resistance Level
2. Vanilla RSI
3. 2-period RSI
4. Centreline Crossover
5. RSI Double Bottom
6. Price/RSI Divergence
7. RSI Inverted Head & Shoulders
8. RSI Resistance Trendline Breakout
9. RSI Trendline Support
10. RSI + Bullish Engulfing
11. RSI + MACD
12. Positive Reversal
13. RSI + Price Channel
14. RSI + Moving Averages
15. RSI + Bollinger Band
16. RSI + Moving Averages
17. RSI + 20 SMA
18. 9-day RSI Average Crossover
19. RSI + Stochastic + MA
20. RSI + CCI

In fact, there can be *dozens* of ways to trade with RSI.

In this chapter, you will find 20 popular trading strategies, where traders use RSI to their advantage, either independently or with the help of some other tool/indicator.

Look at them, check them and if you find any of them appealing, backtest and update your trading strategy arsenal.

RSI alone is a mighty force, but it has so many facets that we can easily misunderstand its message. I am often so preoccupied with divergences, that due to my focus on them I miss noticing reversals till it is too late.

This is why it is necessary to confirm RSI signals by other indicators or signals, though frankly speaking I don't think that Moving Averages can help here. As we have already discussed, moving averages are lagging indicators, while RSI is a leading indicator. However these eight confirmation tools are generally used in RSI trading:

1. Price trendline and RSI trendline (for finding support and resistance levels)
2. Horizontal support and resistance level (because price has a memory)
3. Bollinger Bands
4. Moving average crossover
5. Moving Average of RSI itself
6. Bullish or bearish candles at critical junctures
7. Higher timeframe chart
8. Volume

'Volume tends to build when prices move in their primary direction; it tends to fall during the counter-trend, during corrections or during pauses in a stock's move.' -Donald L Cassidy

Remember, today most of the trading is done by computers with algorithms by big brokers or banks or big traders. So we have to prepare a solid strategy.

Important tip : Most of the retail traders want 100% success rate, which is impossible in stock market. This is why they don't set stop loss or book losses, but hang on to the losers. They don't have a trade strategy in place; hope is their strategy.

In my opinion, traders should aim at the target of 50% success rate. Be prepared that you will be wrong 5 times out of 10 in your trades. Naturally, this would compel you to make a better strategy, where you will let your winners run and cut short the losers. I also plead guilty here; I should also remember this.

If you don't believe me, at least listen to Andrew Cardwell's advice, ' We're a trader. We go to the market, and we know we're going to try and make profits, we're going to take losses, but you have to be willing to admit when you're wrong because the most successful traders in the world are only right 30% to 40% of the time just like batting title. You're not going to hit a home run every time. You don't try and hit a home run. Try and understand what the market is showing you.'

So here are the 20 popular RSI trading strategies to give you an idea how some other traders make their strategy:

1. RSI + Support/Resistance Level

- 14-period RSI is below 30. (oversold)
- Price is testing a support zone.
- Buy above any bullish price candle/bar.

2. Vanilla RSI

This is the simplest of strategy, this is why it is called vanilla strategy.

- Buy when RSI crosses 30 level from below.
- Exit when RSI reaches near 70 level.

3. 2-Period RSI

The 2-period RSI is the brainchild of Larry Connors. This unconventional lookback period turns the RSI into an incredible short-term timing tool. Traders should look for buying opportunities when 2-period RSI moves below 10.

First, identify the major trend using a long-term moving average; Connors recommends the 200-day moving average. The long-term trend is up when a security is above its 200-day SMA.

Traders should look for buying opportunities when above the 200-day SMA.
Connors advocates exiting long positions on a move above the 5-day SMA.

4. Centreline Crossover

Previously we have seen Vanilla RSI. This is somewhat similar, as it is so basic.

- Whenever RSI crosses centreline of 50 from below, go long.
- When it reaches near 70 level, exit.

5. RSI Double Bottom

This strategy is based on Wilder's Failure Swing concept (W pattern) and partly on bullish divergences. It improves the odds of success, though there is no guarantee that RSI will not ditch you in between.

The first price bottom is made on heavy volume. After the first price sell-off, which also results in a breach of 30 on the RSI, the stock will have a snapback rally.

This rally is short lived and is then followed by another snap back reaction which breaks the low of the first bottom.

This second low is where stops are run from the first reaction low. Shortly after breaking the low by a few ticks, the security begins to rally sharply. This second low not only forms a double bottom on the price chart but the relative strength index as well.

The reason this second rally has legs is for (1) the weak longs were stopped out of their position on the second reaction, and (2) the new shorts are being squeezed out of their position. The combination of these two forces produces sharp rallies in a very short time frame.

6. Price/RSI Divergence

This is a simple and solid strategy, though there are several ifs and buts here.

- Buy, when you find Bullish divergence of RSI, when price makes a fresh low, but RSI does not.

- Sell at bearish price action or at resistance level.

As we have discussed in Chapter 5 on divergences, RSI tends to give multiple divergences, so if you buy on first divergence itself, price may not support your decision. Usually it is safer to buy on second divergence.

7. **RSI Inverted Head &Shoulders**
   - Buy when you see an inverted Head & Shoulders (a bullish trend reversal signal) on RSI panel.
   - Book profit when RSI reaches near 70.
   - For confirmation, buy on bullish candle and on support.

8. **RSI Resistance Trendline Breakout**

When RSI breaks its own resistance trendline, it is time to go long. It is usually safe, yet we should seek confirmation from candles and support as well as resistance levels. Volume can also confirm the RSI breakout.

9. **RSI Trendline Support**
   - Buy, when RSI takes support at its own support line and starts moving up.
   - Close the position, when RSI reaches near 70.

10. **RSI + Bullish Engulfing**
    - Buy when RSI gives oversold signal and leaves this zone AND a bullish engulfing candle appears on chart.
    - Close the position, when RSI reaches near 70.

11. **RSI + MACD**
    - Buy, when the RSI gives a oversold signal, which is supported by a MACD signal line crossing.

- Close the position if either indicator provides an exit signal.

12. Positive Reversal

- In an uptrend buy when you see a positive reversal and after it, the price starts moving up.
- Calculate the profit by the formula provided in this book in Chapter 6 on Reversals.
- Close the position slightly below the projected target.

13. RSI + Price Channel

This strategy can be adopted only in price channels.

- Buy when price bounces from the bottom line of the channel and RSI bounces from its oversold zone.
- Close your position, when price reaches near the upper line of the channel.

14. RSI + Moving Averages

This is used by forex day traders.

Time frame: 1 day

Moving Averages: 5 period EMA & 12 period EMA

Buy, when 5 period EMA crosses the 12 period EMA from below to the upside AND RSI is above 50 level.

15. RSI + Bollinger Band

Day traders use this strategy in 1 minute chart.

Bollinger Band period: 40

RSI period: 6

Buy when price rises from the lower line of Bollinger Band

and RSI increases from 20 levels.

The traditional way of using Bollinger is to trade for reversals. If a price hits the upper or lower band, it is likely to reverse as prices have already reached the extreme end.

Confirmations:

- RSI divergence
- Bullish candlestick patterns

If you are looking to buy, the ideal time would be when the price is at the lower band, RSI is oversold, there is a bullish RSI divergence and the candlestick shows a bullish pattern.

16. RSI + Moving Averages

This strategy is for day trading and it is a RSI/MA crossover entry strategy. It is a small profit, little risk strategy.

In hourly chart (60 minute chart) set RSI to 21 period.

Get a 10 period moving average of the RSI.

Trades are only taken in the direction of the trend, so wait for an uptrend to buy.

- During an uptrend, RSI moves below 40.
- After it, when the RSI crosses back its own moving average (10), go long.
- Close your position, when price moves a little in your favour.

17. RSI + 20 SMA

This is a swing trading strategy, which uses daily chart.
RSI period: 5 days.

- Price has to be above the 20 SMA indicating an uptrend.
- Wait for price to pull down to touch the 20 SMA line.
- Now look at RSI, if it has bottomed below 50 level and has started to turn up.

- This is the buy signal. Take quick profits.

18. 9-day RSI Average Crossover

Here the signal line of 9 day Exponential RSI average is used, about which we have already talked.

Buy, when RSI line crosses its average line from below to the upside.

Close your position after a little profit.

19. RSI + Stochastic + MA

MA: 10 period

Buy when:

- Price is crossing MA from below to up.
- RSI and Stochastic exit oversold zone.

All three signals should be received within three candles, otherwise, they will lose their value.

20. RSI + CCI

RSI period: 30

CCI period: 6

- Buy when RSI is above 50 line and CCI gives -100 crossovers from below.
- Close your position, when RSI crosses the 50 line from above to below.

CHAPTER 10: BREAKING THE MYTH: RSI CAN REMAIN OVERSOLD/OVERBOUGHT FOR SEVERAL MONTHS?

Experts say that in a stock RSI can remain in oversold or overbought zone for several months or even years.

Well, well, it is a myth; it doesn't happen in daily charts.

In my study of daily charts of Nifty index, I didn't find it true. I didn't find a single stock, in which RSI has remained oversold or overbought for more than three months in the daily chart.

- May be, such a thing happens in Forex or commodities.
- Or may be, it happens in operator-driven stocks or circuit stocks like Ruchi Soya.
- Or may be, it happens in higher timeframe charts other than daily chart.

In my study of Nifty 50 stocks for the past 15 years, I found that in WEEKLY chartS, Brittania, Bajaj Auto, GAIL, Grasim, HDFC, HDFC Bank, Hero Moto, HUL, ICICI Bank, Infosys, IOC, ITC, L&T, Mahindra & Mahindra, Maruti, Nestle, Reliance, Shree Cement, TCS, Titan, Vedanta etc. remained in overbought zone for more than 4-6 months at a time.

However, during the same period, RSI didn't remain overbought in their Daily chart.

For example, check the WEEKLY chart of Brittania, in which RSI remained in the overbought zone for 10 months:

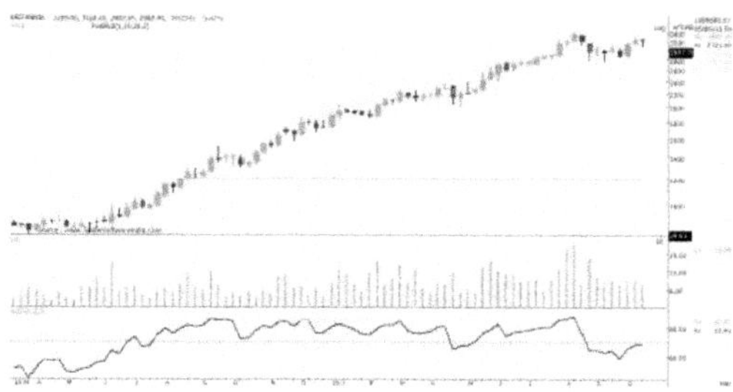

However, in the daily chart it was not in the overbought zone for so long. It kept on crossing the 70 line quite frequently both the ways.

And there was no chart, weekly or daily, where RSI remained in the oversold zone for more than 4 months.

So you see, it was a myth, only because we relied on the experts, who told us about overextended duration, but didn't tell us that it happens only in terms of WEEKLY charts and that too rarely.

In my study of 50 Nifty stocks, I found that it has happened only once or at most twice in the last 15 years. And it happened only in 40% stock charts. So it is quite a rare sight! But yes, it can happen in weekly chart. You see, four months mean 18 candles and it might happen when the atmosphere is quite bullish. But four months mean 90 candles or so in daily chart, so it is not likely to happen. Why so? Because just a small anti-trend movement in price is enough to eject RSI from the overbought zone.

In longer timeframes, RSI can remain in overbought for months (for weekly charts) and for years (in monthly charts), but it happens rarely even there.

CHAPTER 11: ADDITIONAL TIPS

'I've always used three keys to success I talk to people about when I give a presentation—methodology, patience, and discipline. The discipline to follow your rules, stay within your rules, control your emotions; and the patience to, as I quote, say allow the market to show you what it wants to do, not what you want it to do. Well, a lot of people force the issue. Nobody holds a gun to my head to tell me what to trade.' -Andrew Cardwell

- Usually 60-70 levels on RSI are considered overbought, but during breakouts RSI in 60-70 range is considered the best.
- RSI shows the relative strength of a stock, as compared to that stock's historical strength. If RSI is above 60, it means that a stock is strong and it is in a nice position to give a powerful breakout. Breakout needs a lot of power and if a stock is weak, either the breakout would be unsuccessful or it would not prove much profitable. RSI's best level at the time of breakout should be more than 60 and less than 70. Why? Why RSI doesn't give breakouts more often above 70 levels? Why breakouts take place when RSI is generally between 50-70 levels? There is a simple reason behind it. If RSI reaches its overbought 70 level, investors and short-sellers would increase the supply of the stock by selling it. Bulls don't want significant supply of the stock at the time of breakout, which is sure to come if RSI reaches 70, so they sieze the opportunity when RSI is below 70, so that additional supply doesn't upset their breakout plans.
- In my study of descending channel breakouts, I found that 75% of the breakouts occurred when RSI was in the range of 51-70. Whenever you are in a dilemma whether a stock may give breakout or not, look at RSI levels. If RSI is between 51-70,

from bottom with a morning star or morning doji star. If you know this peculiarity, it will help you when Reliance Industries will give a morning star in a downtrend.

Prologue

www.ingramcontent.com/pod-product-compliance
Ingram Content Group UK Ltd.
Pitfield, Milton Keynes, MK11 3LW, UK
UKHW021922190726
13853UKWH00002B/795

9 798889 355816